YOUNG WRITERS

OVER THE MOON

NOTTINGHAMSHIRE

Published in Great Britain in 1997 by
POETRY NOW
1-2 Wainman Road, Woodston,
Peterborough, PE2 7BU

HB ISBN 1 86188 196 7
SB ISBN 1 86188 191 6

Foreword

The *Over The Moon* competition was an overwhelming success - over 43,000 entries were received from 8-11 year olds up and down the country, all written on a wide variety of subjects. Reading all these poems has been a painstaking task - but very enjoyable.

Many of the poems were beautifully illustrated. This just emphasises how much time, effort and thought was put into the work. For me, this makes the editing process so much harder.

I hope that *Over The Moon Nottinghamshire* highlights the diversity of today's young minds. I believe that each of these poems shows a great deal of creativity and imagination. Many of them also express an understanding of the problems, socially and environmentally, that we are all facing.

The poems that follow are all written on different levels, and some are more light-hearted than others. With a considerable variety of subjects and styles, there should be something to appeal to everyone.

Sarah Andrew
Editor

CONTENTS

Jason Bilbie	17
Charlotte Mee	18
Emma Brown	18
Leah Holden	19
Jean Frew	19
Diane Radford	20
Leanne Holland	21
Bradley Wall	21
Jessica Hill	22
Chris Allan	22
Kerie Launders	23
Carly Pickering	24
Howard Dodds	24

Burton Joyce Primary School

Rosie Barnes-Brett	25
Rachel Tivey	25
Andrew Stevenson	26
Hannah Croft	26
Kim Brown	26
Alex Mackereth	27
Simon Birchnall	27
Ryan Springthorpe	28
Arthur Luetkemeier	28
Lucy Rennie	29
Charlotte Reddish	29
Paul Knott	30
Daniel Pacey	30
Steven Faust	31
Emma Mosley &	
Kirsty Pritchett	31
Ricky Turner	32
Martin Klima	32
Joshua Marriott	32
Erica Clothier	33
Bridget Pickerill	34
Natalie Tuffrey &	
Elouise Ashby	34
Matthew Brooks	35

Leo Rodmell	52
Holly Lambert	52
Paul Stock	53
Peter King	53
Laura Gourlay	54
Amy Hulme	54
Mustafa Raniwala	55
Thomas Carter	55
Heather Smith	55
Carl Court	56
Katie Whitlam	56
Rachel Scotton	57
Chris Chiu	57
David Spencer	58
Rowena Ward	58
Wai Ting Chung	59
Samantha Lucas	59
Jennifer Drummond	60

Highfields School

Scott Bennett	60
Julian Heptonstall	61
Chris Allen	61
Keeley Pegg	62
Richard Bombroffe	62
Jordan Lee	63
Merelina Monk	63
Katy Morrison	64
Harriet Applewhite	64
Jessica Hand	65
Kayleigh Hall	65
Josh Rollin	66

John Blow Primary School

Andrew Storey	67

Keyworth Primary & Nursery School

Carla Cockburn	67
Lindsey Frame	68
Vicky Fackrell	68
Rachel Shields	69

	Emma Whitelam	70
	Kym Doughty	70
	Jane Archer	71
	Jane Boston	72
	Kate Allen	72
	Sabina Mulloy	73
Kimberley Primary School		
	Matthew Beadsworth	73
	Alex Brown	74
	Amy Gathercole	74
	Amy Fewster	74
	Hannah Ocheduszko	75
	Kirsty Rowley	75
	Becky Duerden	76
	Julie Rhodes	76
	Jade Edis	77
	Robert Chambers	77
	Rachael Messom	78
	Gary Wood	78
	Ricky Duerden	78
	Jamie Rose	79
	Matthew Watson	79
	Laura Matkin	80
	Kieran Ahern	80
	Charlotte Edwards	81
	Sarah Clarke	81
	Thomas Towlson	82
	Stephanie Crowe	82
	Kayleigh Anderson	83
	Tony Johnson	83
Kinoulton Primary School		
	Robin Colley	84
	Sarah Tyler	84
	Niki Popplewell	85
	Shane Bullivant	85
	Natalie Tomany	86
	Joe Wilkins	86
	Joanne Pinks	87

Rachael Hall	87
Jacob Sanderson	87
Felicity Price	88
Jennifer Salt	88
Stuart Neaves	89

Linby cum Papplewick Primary School

Emma Orton	89
Matthew Turner	90
Cassie Whitehead	90
Steven Sheppard	90
William Burnett	91
Hannah Page	91
Kim Ward	92
Lee March	92
Charlotte Atkin	93

Lowes Wong Junior School

Patrick Dandy	93
Claire Fletcher	94
Rebecca Peacock	94
Harriet Danby	95
Emily Goodwin	95
Lucy Poyzer	96
Jonathan Curtis-Bell	96
Martin Stretch	97
Rachel Watts	97
Catherine Frazer	98
Helen Rajan	98
Victoria Farren	99
Jack Cottam	99
Joanna Ford	100
Claire Undy	100
Christopher Lowe	101
Ben Cowley	101
Alice Moore	102
Alison Wright	102
Chloe Coops	103
Nicholas Sharp	103
Aaron Oliver-Taylor	104

Holliegh Gallon	104
Lauren Hotchkiss	105
Richard Hill	106
James Kirkham	106
Bel Kraay	107
Zoë Ellis	107
Nicola Brown	108
Punam Bhalla	108
Bryony Holt	109
Joshua J M Box	109
Ben Tanner	110
Mark Pearce	110
Aimee Cottam	111
Helen Stark	112
Lucy Hetherington	112
Natalie Wright	113
Edward Hillier	114
Emily Perry	114
Toby Robinson	115
David Proctor	115
Leanne Scothern	116
Jake Hall	117
Paul Thompson &	
Ben Saunders	117
Ben Griffiths	118
Mark Rainbow	118
Hannah Magor	119
Thomas Moor	120
Kate McCallum	120
Bhavni Patel	121
Daniel Huson	121
Grace Moore	122
Rebecca Rennison	122
Christopher Naisbitt	123
Emily Evans	123
Kerri Clay	124

Lynncroft Primary School

Emma Randle	124

Kim Read	125
Lindy Deaton	125
Peter Lowery	126

Manvers Junior School

Nigel Li	126
Bryan Duncan	127
Robin Stevenson	127
Robert Perry	128
Angie Mason	128
Alex Farran	129
Louise Whitehouse	130
Lucy Clark	130
Jonathan Pratt	131
Lee Kirton	132
Rachael Webster	132
Andrew Wilson	133
Richard Sentance	133
Luke Franklin	134
Jo Groom	134
Penny Turns	135
Loren Moyes	136
Andrew Bee	136
Charlotte Thomson	137
Jennifer Clark	138
Lewis Hackett	139
Christian Lewis	139
Craig Hooks	140
Lindsay Durham	140
Amy Baxter	141
Andrew Mudie	141
Louise Green	142
Elizabeth Cowell	143
Matthew Savage	144
John Martin	144

Newlands Junior School

Kirsty Lilliman	145
Michele Froggatt	145
Lee Wood	146

Thomas Hackett	163
Adam Grundy	163
James Morgan, Daniel Blake,	
Jason Oliver, Simon Leonard	164
Chelsea Harris	164
Keisha Makanjuola	165
Kelly Powell	165
Kyle Denoon & Scott Lumley	166
Lindsey Kate Burke	166
Christopher Pearson	167
Mathew Overton	167
Dwane Oakey	168
Sean Rawson	168
Stephen Bullick	169
Elizabeth Mary Abbott	169
Damian Charles Gray	170
Lucy Woodman	170
Michelle Rossitter	171
Sean Hendry	172
Ben Brodsky	172
Craig Norman	173
Adam Denoon	173
Kerrie O'Neill	174
Hollie Morris	174
Victoria Boultby	175
Aaron Tyler	175
John Neale	176
Kevin Haw	176
Alex Lindley	177
Natasha Dames	177
Emma Roberts	178
Marc Stone	178
Rebecca Doubleday	179
Anthony Bullick	179
Dean Wheatley	180
Jacqueline Smith	180

Rise Park Junior School

Sally Cullis	181

Aimee Mitchell	181
Rachael Beeson	182
Tara Ricketts	182
Andrew Makings	183
Adil Lone	183
Charlotte Foster	184
Claire Millington	184
Scott Smith	185
Steven Pinegar	185
Claire Fiona Stimpson	186
Richard Crofts	186
Kayleigh Garratt	187
Rachael Stephenson	187
Craig Stewart	188
Daniel Whittingham	188
Laura Johnson	188
Jennifer Houghton	189
Adrian Swann	189
Mark Clayton	190
Gemma Harrison	190
Anthony Archer	191
Tara Broady	191
Carly Stephenson	192
Priya Saggar	192
Tony Curtis	193
Claire Dale	193
Heather Cree	194
Matthew Wales	194
Jamie Heimour	195
Darren Watson	195
Lindsey Palmer	196
David Cripwell	197
Lee Bennett	197
Daniel Machin	197

Rufford Junior School

Emma Pyatt	198
Kayleigh Straw &	
Coral Davis	198

	Ashley Robinson	199
	Gemma Shipman	199
St Joseph's School		
	Peter Renwick	199
	Felicity Youngson	200
	Simon Kokoszko	201
	Natasha Brown	202
St Patrick's RC Primary School		
	Lucy Daly	203
St Philip Neri RC School		
	Claire Brown	204
Sneinton C of E Primary School		
	Eleanor Benton-Gunn	204
	Sarah Daoud	205
	Lee Morris	205
Stevenson Junior School		
	Sheli-Anne Robertson	206
	Shelley Thompson	206
	Richard Allum	207
	Rebecca Thorpe	207
	Jonathan Shierbaum	208
	Natalie Fisher	209
Sunnyside Primary School		
	Gareth Davies	210
	Nicola Goodwin	211
	Gina Chapman	212
Tuxford Primary School		
	Claire Dowson	213
	Nicola Wyld	214
	Kim Barker	215
Underwood C of E Primary School		
	Francesca Pursell	216
Walesby Primary School		
	Laura Parsons	216
Whitemoor Primary School		
	Amanda Yates	217
	Sunita Landa	218
	Mahezabin Hirani	219

Willow Farm Primary School

FLY

I was watching the TV when something caught my eye,
I looked at it and then I saw the most annoying fly!
It flew onto the lamp shade, and then around the room.
All I could think to myself is 'That fly has met his doom!'
I stood up, I was angry, in fact I was fuming mad,
I bent down and I picked up . . . the weekly local Chad.
The fly was sitting innocently on my mum's old antique vase.
As I imagined whacking the annoying fly to Mars,
I aimed and then I swatted
'Yes the fly is mashed,'
But then I realised what I had done the antique vase was smashed!
I hid the pieces all away, I thought that, that was it,
Until my mum was hoovering and she found a bit.
I said ' The baby did it!'
She said 'Don't tell me a lie!'
'All right' I said 'I did it, but at least *I killed the fly*!'

Daniel Evans (11)

DRAGONS

See the dragon plod along,
See the tail growing long
The claws are strong
So do not shout
Otherwise he will spit fire out.
Sometimes he is rough
Sometimes he is good,
Look at the dragon in the sky,
I never knew they could fly.

Kylie-Marie Smyth (8)

TIGER

Two piercing eyes,
Gaze intently into my own
Sparkling
Like a thousand sunbeams
On a shady pool.
Powerful muscles
Rippling beneath silken skin
Tense and liquid
Ready to pounce.
Four supple limbs,
Slide easily
Through dappled shade.
The golden sunshine
Imperceptibly merging
With sweeping lines.
A handsome face,
With perfect contours,
Gently curving
Across a heavy forehead,
The graceful animal
Silently slips
Through the swaying grasses.
Suddenly becoming
A natural part of the landscape.

Then the tiger spits
With a ferocious rage
And claws angrily at the steel bars
That lock away
All her terrible beauty.
Why?

Helen Archer (11) Abbey Road Primary School

SUMMERTIME

Sunshine in the sky
Makes the sky so blue and fine.
In the sun we all play
Oh mum, let us stay
Grown-ups sitting in the sun
Most children havin' fun
Oh, thank you, sun.

Gemma Rigby (8) Albany Junior School

HONEY BEAR

There was a bear
Who lived in a cave,
His greatest love was honey.
He had two pence a week
Which he could never save
So he never had any money for honey.
I bought him a money box
red and round,
In which to put his money.
He saved and saved
Till he got a pound,
then he spent it all
On honey, honey.

Natasha Stones (8) Albany Junior School

3

I SIT UP THERE TO SEE

Me and my tree,
I sit up there to see,
The wonderful sight of the sea,
Which can sparkle and shine,
And the tree is lovely and pine,
But the tree is all mine.
Fine but pine.
I wear my green jeans
To match the trees.
Then I could never be happier.

Thomas Burton (9) Albany Junior School

HOW I LIKE JELLY

How I like jelly.
It wobbles like my belly,
Put it on a plate.
Say it was not too late.
Put it on the floor.
Kick it out the door.
Kick it out, kick it out
It will bounce back in the house.

Ryan Hope (9) Albany Junior School

I WISH I WAS AN ASTRONAUT

I wish I was an astronaut,
floating up in space.
But I am not yet old enough,
you know that from my face.

Some day I will be up there,
and I hope you will be with me.
I wish I was an astronaut,
and we could have some tea!

Kane Williams (8) Albany Junior School

SPRINGTIME

Little daffodils dance around
Leaving their petals on the ground
Buttercups yellow, snowdrops white
Dancing in the new daylight.

Around the fields are beautiful trees
With wasps and flies and busy bees
Birds are flying in the skies
Along with beautiful butterflies.

Flowers grow and birds sing
I'm so happy now it's spring.

Stacy Russell (9) Awsworth Junior School

SPRING IS HERE

While leaves begin to grow,
There's a purple sea below,
Snowdrops white, violets blue,
I love spring, don't you?

Buds bloom upon the trees,
While up in the air are buzzing bees,
I love spring it is great,
It's time for all the animals to meet up and mate.

A blanket of snowdrops gleaming white,
While the sun is shining yellow so bright,
The insects are scurrying, scurrying away,
While the horses in the field are eating some hay.

Jo Hosker (10) Awsworth Junior School

SPRING

In the spring flowers grow,
We can say goodbye to all the snow.

In the fields little lambs play,
And all the birds are here to stay.
The days get longer,
The nights get shorter,
So we have to drink,
Lots of water.

Matthew Stanbridge (10) Awsworth Junior School

SPRING

Children start to play in the park,
Laughter is heard with a dog's bark,
Kites are flying,
Children are crying,
Spring is here.

Various games are played in the street,
You can hear the sound of children's feet,
Tapping and turning,
Children learning,
Spring is here!

Lucy Trueman (11) Awsworth Junior School

SPRING

Flowers bloom, birds sing,
What a lovely time is spring,
In the fields little lambs play,
Amongst the grass all day.

Animals begin to waken,
Now don't be mistaken,
Because all the trees are beginning to bloom,
White, blue skies above loom.

Children begin to play in the park,
Laughter is all around and little dogs bark,
While buzzing bees collect pollen,
Everyone is calling.

Rachael Flewitt (10) Awsworth Junior School

7

SPRING

In the fields that are green
Little lambs can be seen
Butterflies flutter round and round
Little twigs fall to the ground.

In a blanket of spring
Hear the bells of the church ring
Little snowdrops that are white
Hear everyone jump for delight.

Little berries that are sweet
Hear the birds go tweet tweet.

Katie Savidge (9) Awsworth Junior School

SPRING

Spring comes to Britain
Swallows come back
Cuckoos return
Spring's green leaves
Clothe the trees
Days get longer
Brighter and warmer
Children playing
In spring's warm air.

Tom Smith (10) Awsworth Junior School

COLOUR

It shines through the dark
whenever I am gloomy
the colour that makes me happy
when I look at you I feel like dancing.
It makes me so joyful I could laugh.
It shines so bright it makes my eyes water
It lights up my way through the dark.

Amy Wardle (9) Blessed Robert Widmerpool RC Primary School

COLOURS

Deep red, like a petal on a rose,
Blood dripping from a devil's mouth,
A ruby shining in a gold glass case,
A deep red dragon dancing in a Chinese parade.

Katrina Paling (10) Blessed Robert Widmerpool RC Primary School

COLOURS

The sky on a light night
The moon shining down through the trees
A shadow lurking round a corner
A bird flying through the night sky
Car lights streaming round a bend
Sparkling Christmas trees covered with snow
Thunder rumbling across the sky
Glittering diamonds in a dark mist.

Emma J Whitt (10) Blessed Robert Widmerpool RC Primary School

I SHOULD LIKE TO . . .

I should like to see the planet of
love and beauty float in the sky like
a bird in water.
I should like to make the heavens out
of hearts of love, see the sunset cry.
I should like to fly in the sky with
birds' wings. Fire and water shall mix.
I should like to hold the power of
heaven's God, live in life and death.
I should like rainbow drops to cry with
my eyes see flows of love on heaven's flats.

James Want (10) Blessed Robert Widmerpool RC Primary School

AFRAID OF SNAKES

Felt dizzy
Slithering in front of me
Scared
Run fast
Get away
Still dark
Get tired
Keep running
Faster
Faster
Out of woods
Run home
Sit down
Sigh of relief
No snakes.

Liam Daley (8) Bonington Junior School

AFRAID OF THE DARK

Light room
Bulb popped
Door slammed
Darkness came
Frightened
Shiver
Like wind blowing the tree
Started to cry
Shouted mum
Shouted dad
No-one there
Hid
Felt sweaty
Said don't panic
But panicked
Mum back
Dad back
Light back
Not frightened
Safe.

Kerry Limb (8) Bonington Junior School

THE SKY

The sky is beautiful
The sky is bright
The sky is wonderful,
and it's got night.
The sky is beautiful
The sky is bright
The sky's got stars,
and they give light.

Chloe Collier (9) Brookfield Primary School

SPACE

Space, space amazing place,
Rockets whizzing all over the space,
Astronauts gliding,
Aliens riding,
Space, space amazing place,
Aliens all over the place,
Mars, Uranus, Jupiter, Pluto,
Space, space amazing place,
Space is a great place,
Space is a wonderful place.

Danielle Etheridge (10) Brookfield Primary School

SCHOOL

Every Monday morning my teacher says
'I know that!'

Every Tuesday morning my teacher says
'Don't do that!'

Every Wednesday morning my teacher says
'Don't sit on 2 legs of your chair!'

Every Thursday morning my teacher says
'Have you got your old merit badges at home?'

Every Friday morning my teacher says
'Have you brought those merit badges
back?' and everyone in the class shouted
'No!'

Jodie Mee (9) Brookfield Primary School

THE WILLOW TREE

The willow is a weeper and it lays
over the ground,
The birds sleep in its branches,
The night is delicate and the birds
go to sleep,
The wind blows calmly,
The willow sings and sings,
The willow blows happily and the willow
goes to sleep,
The birds are very happy that the
willow did not sing all night.

Amy Parsons (9) Brookfield Primary School

FIREWORKS

Whizzing fireworks in the air,
Gold, red and green,
Bang! Go the rockets
Whoosh goes the jack in the box.
The night is black as coal.
Toffee apples and chocolate ones lovely jubbly.
I like my mum's best,
My dog Tosh he can't come!
I like the sparklers,
and I really like the Catherine wheels.
But then I have to go home
And wait for next year.

Nicola Alich (10) Brookfield Primary School

THE REDS

I support Man U,
They are a cracking team,
Cantona is skilful,
Giggs makes the girls scream.

They say they're ones for the championship,
I really quite agree,
People say 'No they ain't,
Liverpool for me.'

Here comes towering Schmiechel,
Punching the ball away,
Irwin with classic defending,
Paul Parker passing to David May.
They've beaten Bolton 6 - 0,
They've beaten Forest 5 - 0,
The question is, who will stop them now?

I really don't know who will
Liverpool, Newcastle, Aston Villa,
Boro', West Ham and Spurs,
They never ought to be in our league,
Playing like a bunch of girls.
So here I am on this day,
Telling you who is best,
Yes you've guessed it is Man U,
This team will never rest.

Jamie Pickering (9) Brookfield Primary School

FIREWORKS

Fireworks are pretty and bright
Crash
Bang
Bump
Crack
round and round
up and down
curve and slant.
They're so exciting
Some go up into the sky
then come back and land on the
ground.
People scream
        shout
make loud sounds.
Beautiful amazing
colourful lights
make the city beautiful and bright.
Some are long and some are short.
Just make sure you don't get caught,
when they're alight in the night.

Jacqueline Mason (9) Brookfield Primary School

THE BEAR

Big bears give us nightmares
Brown bears tear their way down town
Bears claws big and long
Bears teeth razor sharp
Please don't kill a bear.

Jack Bradley (9) Brookfield Primary School

MANCHESTER UTD
(The world's greatest football club)

Cantona's skilful, Giggs is cool,
No wonder Man U rule.
They're the best, just forget the rest,
Remember to wear a Man U vest.
Alex Ferguson has got the brain
And Man United will always reign,
All the people are here to say
That Man United will win the FA.
The whistle goes,
Giggs runs with the ball
Down the wing, and doesn't stall,
Crosses to Mclair who's in despair,
He heads it in, Man U could win,
But I am not quite sure 'cause here comes Moore.
Holey Moley where's the goalie,
Moore hits the ball, Man U make a wall,
It hits two players in the face, they look a disgrace.
It goes into the back of the net,
Man U are really upset.
But straight away
Man U score, hooray.

Tim Carter (10) Brookfield Primary School

HOW I FEEL ABOUT THE WORLD

I feel the world is a wonderful place,
It's full of wonderful things,
Dogs
Cats
Horses,
Whales,
And thousands more.
I feel the world would be an even better
place if there wasn't any starvation,
Fighting,
Extinction,
Homeless people living on the streets,
War
And pollution in the air that causes
asthma,
The world is a good place because of all
the animals, friends and families,
I love my world.

Stacey Nelson (10) Brookfield Primary School

BIRD BIRD

Bird, bird flying free.
Bird, bird loves me.
Bird, bird flies from the tree.
Bird, bird kiss me.
Bird, bird flying free.

Jason Bilbie (10) Brookfield Primary School

MY GREAT GRAN

My gran's got a motor bike.
She brings it round each day.
When she goes out with my mum,
I take it out to play.

My gran's got a motor bike.
I take it to the shop.
Zooming down the road to
get a drink of pop.

My gran's got a motor bike.
She lets me take it off
to school.
Ploughing through the rose beds.
Breaking every rule?

Charlotte Mee (11) Brookfield Primary School

MY DAD

My dad is really funny.
He laughs just like a bunny.
He sits and drinks his tea
Then switches on the big TV.
Each day he goes to work,
Comes back covered in dirt.
My dad is rather nice you see
He loves us all especially me.

Emma Brown (11) Brookfield Primary School

MY DAD

My dad fancies a really fat girl
With a big and brownish horrible curl.
He buys her flowers every day
Oh! And by the way her name is Kay.

I don't like her not one bit.
All she does is eat and sit.
Her cheeks are glossy red as roses,
And in the mirror she always poses.

My mum will be raging like a gas fire,
Knowing my dad he's nothing but a drab liar.
There is only one way, only one course,
Ending it all in a drastic divorce.

Leah Holden (10) Brookfield Primary School

VEG

I hate veg,
Don't ask me why,
When I eat them I want to cry.

Veg are gross!
Not nice at all!
One more taste and I will bawl!

I don't like them
Just ask Reg.
I hate veg!

Jean Frew (10) Brookfield Primary School

YUM YUM WHAT'S FOR DINNER?

What's for dinner?
Baked beans and bread
Spiders and flies
(I hope they're all dead)

What's for dinner?
Tomatoes and eggs
Frogs and toads and
Tarantula's legs.

What's for dinner?
Dragons' skin
Cottage cheese and
A fish's fin.

What's for dinner?
Peas in a pod
Snakes' skin and
A slice of cod.

What's for dinner?
I don't know
I feel sick
Toilet, quick, quick, quick!

Diane Radford (11) Brookfield Primary School

MY CAKE

When it was my birthday
I had a birthday cake
And for my present I had a rubber snake.

When it was my birthday
I had a birthday cake
And for my present I went to the lake.

When it was my party
I ate lots of currant buns
And when we had the karaoke
I had a lot of fun.

When it was my birthday
I had a birthday cake
And when I blew my candles out
I knew that I was eight.

Leanne Holland (8) Brookfield Primary School

BRECKEN

My pony's very fluffy,
He has a lot of hairs,
He likes some of the mares!
Then I ride my pony,
When I jump
I scream with laughter
Then land with a shock.
And ride on
Until I'm gone.

Bradley Wall (9) Brookfield Primary School

HOMEWORK

I love to do my homework
I do it every night
I like to do what my teacher says
And I like to do it right.

I love to do my tables
I practise them every night
I like to say them to my mum
And I like to say them right.

I love to read my books
I read them every night
I like to read to my mum and dad
And I like to read them right.

Jessica Hill (9) Brookfield Primary School

MY CAT

Look at my cat
Laying on the floor
Before he goes to bed
He pushes the door.
Look at my cat
Eating his food
Drinking his milk
He's in a bad mood.
Look at my cat
Sleeping all day
He might sleep
Till the end of May.

Chris Allan (9) Brookfield Primary School

FOOTBALL MAD

Sunday afternoon watching football
Arsenal versus Man U.
Oh no
Man U have just scored.
Andy Cole
Wright has the ball
Passes it to Bergkamp
Tries to shoot
It goes in!
A goal by Bergkamp
Half-time
I'm getting worried
I think Man U
are going to win.
Arsenal's got the ball
Marshall gets there,
passes it to Merson
Tries to shoot
It hits the crossbar
Corner to Arsenal
Corner from Platt
Wright headed it in!
Arsenal 2
Man U 1
Final score.

Kerie Launders (9) Brookfield Primary School

DOGS

Dogs on the street
Dogs on the playground
Dogs in the park
Drinking picnic tea.

Dogs in the wood
Dogs racing round
Dogs fetching sticks
Having lots of fun.

Carly Pickering (8) Brookfield Primary School

FOOTBALL MAD

Saturday afternoon
Arsenal v West Ham
First half.
Ian Wright on the ball
Takes a shot and scores.
Half-time.
I am confident
Second half
Platt to Wright to Bergkamp
Takes a shot and scores.
Full time
Arsenal 2 West Ham 0.

Howard Dodds (8) Brookfield Primary School

SPIDER

Spider, spider give me your jewel,
A silver plate with flies for you.
I love the way you're quick and slick,
You climb up on a silver stick,
It is as if you are the king,
You creeply crawly round the house,
Those flies better watch out.

You are as black as black as night,
Your legs are as soft as man's hair,
I love you dearly so don't be scared,
You are not as scary as men say,
You are my friend so please do stay.

Rosie Barnes-Brett (9) Burton Joyce Primary School

NEPTUNE

Neptune is the god of sea,
The sea is stronger than you and me,
But sometimes the sea is quiet and calm,
As it ripples up on the beach of sand,
But when it's rough the waves are grand.

The sea is green,
The sea is blue,
And near the shore it's sometimes
see-through,
The sea can be calm and safe to swim,
But when it's rough it's easy to drown in.

Rachel Tivey (9) Burton Joyce Primary School

FIRE

Fire is angry,
Fire is nice,
Fire is a great bringer of life,
It's sometimes yellow, sometimes red
Let fire burn brightly, Vesta had said.
Let it burn and light will reign,
Over dark again.

Andrew Stevenson (9) Burton Joyce Primary School

GODDESS OF FIRE

Vesta the goddess of fire,
Vesta so bright at night,
Vesta flames so high,
A circle of fire by your side.
It's like a circle of life,
So high and bright in the sky,
Red, orange and yellow flames.

Hannah Croft (8) Burton Joyce Primary School

THE COUNTRYSIDE

The countryside, the countryside a peaceful place,
I walk in the woods and look at the trees,
I look on the ground and see the leaves.
When I walk the leaves all crunch,
I sit on a log and eat my lunch.
The air, the air all fresh and clean,
I look at strange animals I've never seen.

Kim Brown (10) Burton Joyce Primary School

26

SNAKE

The snake with a scaly skin,
Has teeth as sharp as a pin,
He slithers along,
Singing his song,
I've got a big prize to win.

He slithers along the ground,
He slithers without a sound,
He kills the mouse,
Then goes back to his house,
And what a big meal he's found.

Alex Mackereth (8) Burton Joyce Primary School

POEM ABOUT CAVES

Slowly the water dripping down, quiet, quiet,
The mouth of the cave would be a dark, dark place,
It looks so creepy and frightening,
Water dripping, heart thumping, head banging, bats flying,
All part of a cave, with nothing there,
A part of a cave that is still a very dark place indeed,
People shouting, people's echoes,
But it is still a creepy place to be,
The water dripping sounds just soothing,
Water dripping looking like crystals,
Hearing footsteps coming closer,
But no shapes are there,
Stalactites and stalagmites shining like a diamond,
But the cave mouth is still dark.

Simon Birchnall (10) Burton Joyce Primary School

AIN'T TRIPS BRILLIANT!

Ain't sick messy!
Ain't birds got good aims!
Ain't trip food delicious!
Ain't arcades wicked!
Ain't knock and run wicked!
Ain't youth hostels old!
Ain't toilets dirty!
Ain't beans breezy!
Ain't walks torture!
Ain't trips brilliant!

Ryan Springthorpe (10) Burton Joyce Primary School

THE SEA

The sea.
Sometimes scary as can be
Lapping, licking away the sand
On the rocks I do stand
The sea is gargantuan as it overpowers me
A tremendous sight I do see
The sea.
The sea is enormous
It covers three quarters of the earth
It's near Tokyo, Calais and even Perth
Its powerful waves crashing against a cliff
If that was near me it would be certain death.

Arthur Luetkemeier (11) Burton Joyce Primary School

THE PIGLET

A little wrinkled nose
And his tiny small toes
He has quite a little belly
He is very smelly.

He eats a lot of food
He's always in a good mood
He's quiet clever
And he loves hot weather

He loves muck
And he has good luck
He has a curly tail
He leaves a little trail.

Lucy Rennie (10) Burton Joyce Primary School

SKEGGY HERE WE COME

Banging on the window,
waving to your mum,
shouting, screaming, come on, come on, come on.
Finally you're there,
feet banging, scrambling off the coach.
Everyone running to the sea,
splashing, shouting, screaming
to get to the sea first.
At last it's time to go home,
the sun is down the moon is in sight.
Tired children lay on the sand
dreaming of the day ahead.

Charlotte Reddish (9) Burton Joyce Primary School

THE MOON

The moon is shining on the earth below
And spots a blackbird flying low
A nearby forest is very dark
And in a tree there is a lark.
Out of a bush a rat scurries by
With a silver claw and a silver eye.
In a gleaming field there is a plough
And the moon floats on behind a cloud.
The earth goes black
The night is over
Then the sun comes back.

Paul Knott (10) Burton Joyce Primary School

THE SEA

The sea is a very powerful thing,
crashing against the cliffs.
The mighty waves knock me over,
and drag me into the sea.
The refreshing feeling of being in the sea,
The cold feeling of being in the sea.
The forceful waves drag me out further,
The enormous waves crash on my head.

The sea is calm and I'm back home,
the tide is out no harm was done.

Daniel Pacey (11) Burton Joyce Primary School

I'NT TRIPS BRILLIANT

I'nt trips brilliant when you forget to bring your sandwiches home.
I'nt trips brilliant when you don't have to wash for the whole trip.
I'nt trips brilliant when you can go to sleep late.
I'nt trips brilliant when you can get away from your family.
I'nt trips brilliant when you can eat loads of sweets.
I'nt trips brilliant when teachers aren't worried about you getting
work done.
I'nt trips brilliant when you don't have to decide where to go.
I'nt trips brilliant when you can be sick on the bus.

Yes trips are brilliant.

Steven Faust (10) Burton Joyce Primary School

FRIENDS

Me and her we've been best friends for about 2 years.
Even though we fall out a lot.
We always make friends in the end.
So what should you do if you fall out with a friend?
Don't call each other names.
Don't kick each other.
Don't pull each other's hair.
Just shake hands together and make-up.
That's the best thing to do.

Because we are friends.

Emma Mosley & Kirsty Pritchett (10) Burton Joyce Primary School

TIGER

Powerful, pouncer
stalking, stripy beast
mean eyes burning bright
fierce killer of the night.

Ricky Turner (9) Burton Joyce Primary School

INVASION

An invasion.
Sword against sword.
Glaring in the sky.
Screams and cries,
blood on swords.
Spears fly through the sky.

Martin Klima (9) Burton Joyce Primary School

TIGER

Tiger in the jungle hunting all the day,
When he's got his dinner then he'll go away.

Eating in the daylight,
The burning sun is too bright.

Stripping meat from the bone,
As he eats it very slow.

Joshua Marriott (7) Burton Joyce Primary School

MY CATS

My cat was white,
She woke me in the night,
My cat was naughty,
She ran into the road,
Got squashed by a car,
That looked like a toad,
And then she was buried,
At the end of my garden.
Boo hoo hoo!

We still had another cat,
She was furry and fat,
Her stripes were white and black,
She had a little old back,
She would sleep all the day,
She would not play,
Until one day, she was getting old,
In the night 'twas very cold,
My dad came home,
And ran over her leg,
In the morning we were very scared,
She had broken her leg, paralysed her tail,
She was looking very old and frail,
The vet was very worried about her,
The last time I could hear her purr,
Was yesterday.

Erica Clothier (11) Burton Joyce Primary School

STEAM TRAINS

Whoo! Whoo! Whoo! Goes the whistle on the train,
     Ch ch ch ch ch ch! There it goes again.
Under a tunnel the whistle starts to blow,
     All the sounds of the train start to echo.
Hissss says the engine as it comes to a stop,
     Off you get says the master, hoppity hop.
Slowly the steam train puffs away,
     Ready to work for another long day.
Early in the morning the train rushes past,
     Chugging along very, very fast.

Bridget Pickerill (10) Burton Joyce Primary School

THE TRENDY ROCKPOOL

The trendy rockpool
spilling
crashing
searching
bashing
Goes the water against the rocks.
Slimy, slushy, gooey seaweed
Surfing in and out of people's socks.

Lots of bubbles in the pool
it looks really cool.
Weaving in and out finding new places
And people tripping over their laces.

Natalie Tuffrey & Elouise Ashby (11) Burton Joyce Primary School

VESTA GODDESS OF FIRE

Fire burning brightly and being very lively,
burning like a hive of bees, dropping honey on the
leaves, let the fire burn so bright, said Vesta the goddess
who made its light.

Matthew Brooks (8) Burton Joyce Primary School

THE MOON AT NIGHT

Here is the great blue sky,
All of a sudden, gone, in the wink of an eye,
Nocturnal creatures, gathering food and drink,
We stop to think, but in a wink,
All is gone, everything from,
Our camp from night, oh what a fright,
The wind has started howling round,
Never touching the silvery ground,
The stars and the moon, they never fade,
Just as well everything stayed,
Silvery cold, silvery old,
The river gliding by,
Crinkly branches in the sky,
All of these and silver logs,
Looking like some silver hogs,
All of this and much, much more,
Projected by the moon at night.

Karl Brown (11) Burton Joyce Primary School

MOONLIGHT

Glistening water of a silver stream
Silent apart from the graceful sweeping birds
No movement but the moon
All the world silver
And the silver waving corn sways in the gentle breeze
The trees, the grass baste in the moon light.

Adam Vowes (10) Burton Joyce Primary School

A MOONLIT NIGHT

The moon glistening on a very clear night
It looked as if it used all its might
Turning things silver and white
It looked such a wonderful sight.

A silver bird flies in the sky
And on the ground a mouse goes scurrying by.
The long running stream
Turns silver from the moon's beams.

The moon glows on trees
It glows on grass and on leaves
Until at last the moon goes away
For it is another day.

Sarah Allsop (11) Burton Joyce Primary School

36

NOISE

Martin likes trains they go Choo Choo!
Craig likes boats they go Chug Chug!
Matthew likes aeroplanes they go Neeoowww!
Gary likes lorries they go Brum Brum Brum!
But Mrs Mcewen and Mrs Hunt like hot air
balloons because they go Sssh, Sssh Sssh!
Zoe like trains they go Woo Woo!
Ian likes cars they go Beep Beep!
Alia likes buses they go Brum Brum Brum!
But Mrs Brock, Lorraine and Jackie like hot air
balloons because they go ?????

Class 3 : Carlton Digby School

DOWN IN THE DUNGEONS

In the dungeons below the ground
Spooky faced creatures glance around
In the corner under the chair
Crash! Oh I wish I was up there.

These giant beings make me feel so small
The miraculous masks are oh so tall
Shadows swarm above my head
Could they be ghosts brought back from the dead?

Black cats creep about
I wish somebody would let me out
Evil eyes shining bright
Could this be hell in the middle of the night?

Tom Woolley (10) Gotham Primary School

WOMAN WEEPING

A face of a million pieces, behind each piece
There's a story, a story of love
A story of hate, a story for every occasion
Today's story is of a broken heart
A heart feeling love, hate and pain
Her loved one did leave her
Now she is alone
With no-one to care for, no-one to blame
She says her life is in pieces
There is no point to live
If there is a heaven that's where I will be led
Then three days later her body was found
Dead and numb, alone on the ground

Charlotte Riley (11) Gotham Primary School

METAMORPHOSIS OF NARCISSUS

Nimbus clouds wisping about in a great turmoil of action
A pond with no movement breaking the thin film-like surface
The sun rising above the jagged mountains in the far distance
In a land where all things mythical and real live together in
perfect harmony
In a land where the sun and the moon come together to paint
the sky, the most amazing colours and hues
Now, in the world of change, a great feat:
The great god Narcissus is stirred to finally waken
from his deep slumber
Out of the pond and into the wide world metamorphosis
takes place and into man-form he changes
And there in the cave of fantasy he dwells ad infinitum.

Ruth Larbey (11) Gotham Primary School

THE DOG AND I

I was sitting on the bank underneath the shade
A dog came along and drank my lemonade
I chased it off down to the bin
It must have been so scared 'cause it jumped right in
I jumped in after it we had such a fight
I tried to get out and it gave me a bite
I ran off home back to my mum
She said 'That's typical' and whacked me on the bum!

Philip Holbrook (11) Gotham Primary School

THE MUSE

A distracted woman wondering in her mind
focusing on a picture
Painting reflections of a surprising world
Visions engage on people around her
Silencing the distorted dream.

Stephanie Rostron (11) Gotham Primary School

TRANQUILLITY

A warm summer morning
As peaceful as a cool stream, flowing quietly
The never-ending reflection has seen so much
The bridge was once alive with activity
Birds singing in the green, lonely weeping willow trees
The old dull yellow villa standing in silence
The decrepid boat moans across the still stream.

Emma Coppin (11) Gotham Primary School

THE HOUSE WITH THE CRACKED WALLS

The sun beaming brightly over the dried lands,
Angry mosquitoes hungrily searching for their taste of red blood,
The olive trees busting full of fruit,
All of this surrounds the house with the cracked walls

The empty stillness of the blue skies hovering,
Bare rocks bursting through the parched landscape,
Starving grass yearning for water,
Geckos seeking shelter from the harsh sun,
Deep within the shade of the house with the cracked walls.

Kelly Banks (11) Gotham Primary School

WHEN?

As I look down from the cliffs the waves crashed
on the jagged and unfriendly rocks.
I was waiting,
Waiting for my long lost friend

She had written
Written a long and heartbreaking letter
Saying that she was coming
Or trying to come.
It said she might not make it

It began to rain
I clutched the letter in my hand
as I put my hood up.
I was cold
Cold from the strong wind.
The waves were crashing on the rocks
I began to realise why she might not make it.

Eleanor Kemp (11) Gotham Primary School

40

COOL

On a warm autumn day
The ponies came to play
In the long moist grass
And the sky blue pool
Splashing themselves
To try to keep cool
The soft winds blew
Through the rich brown trees
Swaying gently in the breeze
The horse enjoyed being wild and free
But could be ridden by you and me.

Rebecca Vickery (11) Gotham Primary School

THE GHOST NEXT DOOR

The ghost next door is such a bore until I find a clue
What will I do?
I go to the loo and find my queue to start looking for Tracy's backpacks
I've found nothing
I climb out the window and up the tree and find a flea and on
the roof to find some proof there is a ghost!
I climb through and I find a flea on a pea and on the pea is
a leaf there is some teeth!
Then and only then I saw something flying through the air
then I saw a pear flying through the air!
I screamed I ran back up the tree and I saw the
pea I went back in the loo and I found the clue I'm safe.

Andrew Gourlay (8) Greythorn Primary School

NO

Ah! That's not fair you get to go to the zoo can I come too?

No!

Ah! That's not fair you get to go swimming for your party
Can I come too?

No!

Ah! That's not fair you get to go on holiday can I come too?

No!

No no no is there anything I can do?

Yes

What?

You can shut up!

Frances Faye Hunter (8) Greythorn Primary School

JELLY

Jiggly skwiggly
Wiggly guggly
Licky sticky licky picky
Glidy slidy midy tidy
Lubby gubby simply lovely
Lidy sidy midy tidy
Yiggly giggle jeggly migly.

Jodie Lee Haspey (7) Greythorn Primary School

ICE

You put it on your head ouch!
Polar bears make their homes in it.
I like it because you can make a *snowman*
with it.
On nice summer days you can put it in
your drinks.
In winter you can slide all over it and on snow,
Ice is *cold definitely!*
In the winter the pond's surface turns
into ice and the road's surface turns into ice.
If you feel really hot *ice* lollies can cool you
down. (And fans)

Jonathan Wheeler (9) Greythorn Primary School

GOSH

Something going through the ground
shivering and shaking going through the door.
Shivering and shaking in the kitchen.
Bang as some kettles fall on the floor.
Now it's in the dining room making a funny noise.

OOOO!

Now it sounds like it is in the living room
howling and hooting coming up the stairs.
Going in the bathroom mess with the soap
turning on the taps.
Swooping through my door flying over me
Help!

Jack Matthews (8) Greythorn Primary School

PLANES

Planes,
Soaring,
Whizzing,
Flying through the sky.

Swooping,
Diving,
Flying through the sky.

Gliding,
Climbing,
Flying through the sky.

Twisting,
Turning,
Flying through the sky, planes.

James M Bradley (8) Greythorn Primary School

RACING CARS

The race starts.
Cars going fast
Round the corners
Some cars crashing Bang! Bang!
Spinning cars
Crashing then spinning in the air.
Then cars overtake! Overtake!
Sometimes crashing
Then one goes past the chequered flag.
And wins the race.

Leith Gibson (8) Greythorn Primary School

THE CAT ON THE MAT

The cat was sitting
On the mat
Until Andy gives it a hat
Then it turned off the mat
And off flew the hat
So the cat climbed back on the mat.

Anthony Cooper (7) Greythorn Primary School

LIZARD

There was a big lizard. He had big teeth
And big legs
He had a big hard tail
He had sharp spikes on his back
He had big eyes
He was frightening
I ran away.

Sunil Dhund (9) Greythorn Primary School

THE SUN AND THE STARS

The sun and the stars are up
past Mars
Sun in the day stars in the night
Sparkly night they are always a
pretty sight.
Just the sun and the stars.

Nicola Carter (8) Greythorn Primary School

PARENTS

Most people have parents.
A mum or a dad.
Who are loving and caring.
But sometimes get mad,
Though they shout and make us cry,
We love them still and that's not
a lie.
What would we do without parents?
Parents who needs them.

Me!

Charmaine Gill (9) Greythorn Primary School

PIZZA HUT

I once went to a Pizza Hut.
And a pizza hut it was.
I had a lovely pizza.
And a lovely pizza it was.
When I went home I
didn't have the keys.
And so I went back to
the Pizza Hut.
But when I got to the
door the sign said
closed.

Charlotte Ridley (8) Greythorn Primary School

SNOWFLAKES

A snowflake falls gently down on me.
It was cold against my skin.
It was so pretty,
Then! Two, three, four, five, six,
a thousand.
There they were white and silver all over.

I walked around the garden.
'Crunch', goes the snow,
As I stumble through the cold, fluffy powder.

I made a little snowball,
and rolled it round and round.
It got bigger and bigger,
Until I had to sit down.

My snowman's nearly ready,
I've done his hat, his eyes, his mouth,
I know there's something missing,
'The nose!' I will get a carrot from the house.

Alex Archibald (7) Greythorn Primary School

DAY AND NIGHT

Day and night what a
beautiful sight whatever
the weather, it's lovely all the
time. I wish it was all mine.
In sunny Spain or under rain
I don't care where I live as long
as it's not space!

Laura Clayworth (8) Greythorn Primary School

LITTLE BIRDY

I have a little birdy
I keep it in a cage,
I don't think it is happy there.
It's always in a rage.
Once I let it out
of its little cage,
I was hoping to
revive it from its terrible rage.
I made a big mistake
it flew out of the
window now all I
have left is an empty
      cage.

Paul Underwood (9) Greythorn Primary School

ANIMAL ALLITERATION

One walking worm walked to Wales.
Two terrified tarantulas tried tealeaf tea.
Three threatening tigers tried to teach Tywan.
Four fish fried fresh filled fleas.
Five fleas flicked furry fire on fried fish.
Six slithering snakes sat and sizzled sausages.
Seven silly snails sat on slugs.
Eight eating elephants eat every egg.
Nine noiseless nits never naughty.
Ten turning turtles took terrified twins to town.

Nicki Challinger (9) Greythorn Primary School

FRUIT!

Fruit is yum
Ripe or not, always much better than bubble gum!
Unique in every way I'd rather eat a guava any day!
I love to eat mango much better than fizzy pop tango
Thanks, tree you have really pleased me.

Indigo plums, purple and blue too, all of them taste brill!
Strawberries, so sweet, too good to eat!

Grapes make me feel great! But,
Really, nothing can compare with a nice, sweet juicy pear!
Eating orange, what luxury,
Apples, how scrummy!
Tangerines, love at first sight! I could eat fruit all night! So, if
            you see some fruit, go get me! Then as I eat it watch
            my taste buds suck with glee!

Juliet Langton (8) Greythorn Primary School

LEGOLAND

L ego is wonderful Lego is
E verywhere you go in the shops
      you can
G et firemen Lego police Lego you can get
O ctupus Lego monster Lego it's
L ovely to play with it's
A bsolutely *Fabulous*
N othing is better than Lego
D id I mention that I would die
      if I didn't have Lego?

Jack Kevin Smith (8) Greythorn Primary School

CEREALS

Cereal, cereal, can't get enough
my favourite of all are Sugar Puffs.
When we run out and I'm in a fix
that's when I have some Weetabix.
When outside is as cold as a fridge
that's when I have piping hot porridge.
When mummy is busy making some cakes
that's when I have some crunchy cornflakes.
When I want lots of energy to gain
that's when I have some Kellogg's Sustain.
When I am not feeling totally tops
I have a large bowl of Coco Pops.
Chex Chex, are very swell
but I like lots of other cereals as well.
Like, Wheatflakes, Crispies, Shredded Wheat and Bran ,
and if there's nothing else, I'll try Alpen.

Christopher Davies (9) Greythorn Primary School

THING

That thing over there,
Has an awful stare,
It's brown and yuck,
It stinks of muck.

That thing coming near,
Has made an awful smear,
On my bed,
Can't I just chop off his head?

That thing has a mother,
That thing is my
        Brother!

Amy Dolan (10) Greythorn Primary School

VAMPIRE'S HEAD

A swish of black,
A drop of red,
Two yellow eyes,
I drop dead.

A wave of steam,
Some potion bottles,
Purple liquid,
A pot of peas,

A swish of black,
A drop of red,
Two yellow eyes,
And a vampire's head.

Thomas Dykes (9) Greythorn Primary School

THE SLIMY SLUG

The slimy slug,
Looks like a bug
Eating apple pie.

Will he live,
Or will he die
Eating up the apple pie.

The slimy slug,
Looks like a bug,
Eating apple pie
Did he live or
Did he die nobody knows
Because that's a lie!

Gemma McLoughlin (10) Greythorn Primary School

FOOTBALL

Football is cool!
Oh what a foul!
Oh free kick!
Take the corner.
Britton passes the ball to Rodmell. He scores.
And the 'Reds' win.
Limping off the pitch.
Long live the 'Reds'.

Leo Rodmell (9) Greythorn Primary School

FRED MY FRIEND

This is the story
Of Fred my friend
He played on the street
And went in to eat
At bedtime he dreamed
And woke up and screamed
He thought he was dead
And then went back to bed
In the morning he played
With Arny and Dave
He ran in front of a car
And got knocked very far
He could not be saved
And now he lays in a grave.

Holly Lambert (10) Greythorn Primary School

THE FIRE BELL

For years it sleeps in peace
Until its home alights
The bell wakes with a sudden excitement
Banging its head against the round walls trying
to escape.
Everyone around hears the bell
They run outside
The bell has saved them
But they just leave the bell to sleep.

Paul Stock (11) Greythorn Primary School

MY MUM

Tidy your bedroom. Pick up that,
I'm going to go boom if
you don't do that.
What about that picture?
It's on the floor,
In a heap by the bedroom
door.
Those shoes,
that hat.
I really think I should
groom the cat.
You're grounded now.
Thanks mum, you're a pal.
And I'm so so sad!
Mum, your bedroom's just as bad!

Peter King (10) Greythorn Primary School

NONSENSE

Females and males
Girls and boys
Babies and toddlers
And all your little toys,
I come before you
To stand behind you
To tell you a story
I know nothing about.
Late Thursday night
Early Friday morning
An empty truck
Full of bricks
Pulled into my front yard
Killing my cat in the back yard
That same night
Two boys got up to fight
A deaf policeman heard the noise
Came and shot the two dead boys
If you don't believe
This lie is true
Ask the blind man
He saw it too.

Laura Gourlay (10) Greythorn Primary School

LITTLE LIGHT BOX

Little box wrapped up tight,
Deep inside a yellow light.
Rip off the paper
Mummy says later,
Little box left till tonight.

Amy Hulme (9) Greythorn Primary School

STARS

When I look up at the stars my mind goes completely blank
I think of all the constellation waiting to be seen
Suddenly a comet flies past so beautiful and bright
Then the moon comes out like a torch shining at you
Then the sun comes intercepting the moon
But then another night will come and the stars will come out again.

Mustafa Raniwala (10) Greythorn Primary School

THERE WAS A YOUNG LION

There was a young lion
called Hugh
who went to the neighbouring zoo.
He opened up wide
and said
come on inside
and bring the whole family
too.

Thomas Carter (10) Greythorn Primary School

GARDENS

Winter's coming
Ivy leaves
Lots of heathers
Lots of leaves
Big trees swaying
Left to right
Trying not to with all their might.

Heather Smith (10) Greythorn Primary School

BANANAS

Bananas are yellow,
They are curved like crescent moons,
They are textured like fudge but not
juicy like fruit,
Bananas can be purple when they are
bruised,
Bananas are tasty and they're nice to
eat,
But!
Never eat a banana sideways.

Carl Court (11) Greythorn Primary School

MIDNIGHT FOX

She quietly crept
Her nose twitching
Out she creeps
Pricking her ears
She hears a quiet breathing sound
On she creeps silently behind her prey
She pounces on it killing it instantly
Carrying it triumphantly back to her
den
She took one last look around
Her tail flicked and she disappeared.

Katie Whitlam (9) Greythorn Primary School

THE NEW TEACHER

Teacher why have you got such big eyes?
All the better to see round corners in the cloakrooms.

Teacher why does your nose light up?
It only lights up if anyone has a fag round the back
of the shed.

Teacher why do you have such big teeth?
All the better to eat sweets, apples, school dinners
and sometimes children.

So be good little children or I'll
    eat you up.

Rachel Scotton (9) Greythorn Primary School

THE MOON

The moon
It's a creamy coloured balloon.
The moon
It's a ghost, never come alive again.
The stars
Shine around the moon.
Like a movie star with little lights shining
around it.
The moon.

Chris Chiu (11) Greythorn Primary School

THE DOOR

Walking along we pass the door,
Spooky ready to eat someone in the darkness of the night.
The blackness is ready to swallow you,
With the silence of the night.
The door flung open like a gun firing,
Swallowing the silence,
Then bang like an explosion it closes,
No bang no nothing just silence.

David Spencer (10) Greythorn Primary School

THE SEA

The salty sea, sand, slips between my
toes and fingers.

The crashing waves bring fishes to my sea,
The salty sea slip with its fishes dive and dip,
with seaweed backs and gleaming eyes.

The air is full of seagulls' cries,
who are eating the fish with the gleaming eyes.

The dolphins come to eat the food the seagulls drop,
who eat the fish with the gleaming eyes,
all in my salty sea sand slip.

Rowena Ward (11) Greythorn Primary School

THE OCEAN

The ocean covering as far as the naked eye can see,
The sunlight touches the water as it sparkles in the distance.
A dolphin broke to the surface disturbing the peaceful and calm water,
With a gentle flick of its tail it disappeared back beneath
                                        the depths of the ocean.
Thousands of creatures lurking beneath the surface,
Some still unknown to mankind,
The ocean is as beautiful as the pearls in the oysters,
As mysterious as the shadows.
The eight legged monster known as the octopus,
Catches its prey and then hides itself in its dark and scary cave.
The sun sets and once again
The ocean is peaceful and quiet.

Wai Ting Chung (11) Greythorn Primary School

DOLPHIN

The sea can see as far as it can see
as a dolphin breaks through the surface
of the water as the sun is shining on the sea
all around the dolphin as its tail flings
the water around it and there is
silence until the next dolphin comes to
the surface.

Samantha Lucas (11) Greythorn Primary School

FROZEN

My hands have gone, they've been cut off, by
Mr Jack Frost.
The VIP to the hated list.
The icicles grow, the temperature's low,
Outside there's a sheet of tissue snow.
Our noses are red, some have fled, but the
brave have stayed.
The mittens are unravelling, the scarves have gone all grey.
My eyes just feel like playschool clay.
Winter go away, summer please come and stay.

Jennifer Drummond (11) Greythorn Primary School

A LITTLE NEST

There's blackbirds in nan's garden
busy building nests.
They really do work very hard
and never seem to rest.

They're building for their little ones
a home that's soft and warm.
High up in the bushes away from any harm.

Those babies are so lovely
all fluffy and cuddly.
With eyes that sparkle like the stars.
If only they could fly that *far!*

Scott Bennett (9) Highfields School

WHEN I'M ANGRY

When I'm angry I feel like
shouting.
When I'm angry I feel like
breaking something but
I know I shouldn't
I grit my teeth and clench
my fists.

I feel angry when I'm not
allowed to do what I want.
Then I go to my room and have
a tantrum.
Then I forget why I was
angry in the first place.

Sometimes when I'm angry
at myself I feel like crying.
I go to my room and think
about it, then I come
downstairs and say
'Sorry.'

Julian Heptonstall (9) Highfields School

CURRY

My mother made a curry
She cooked it in a hurry
She made it very hot
And cooked it in a pot

But when we sat to eat
We couldn't stand the heat
Now my mum's curry
Is feeding pigs in Surrey.

Chris Allen (8) Highfields School

ANGER IS

Anger is as red as a red red rose,
I've never thought of it I suppose.
For when I'm angry I scream and shout,
I slam the door and stamp about.

I run to my room which has a sign on the door
that says 'Boys beware'
So that my brother won't go in there.
When my dad asks my mum what the fuss is about,
'Anger, anger!' is all I shout.

Keeley Pegg (8) Highfields School

HOW THE WIND BLOWS

It rushes, it gushes, it howls
It yowls, it blows, it crows
That's how the wind blows.

What does the wind do?
It sweeps, it leaps, it creeps
It weeps, it groans, it moans
That's what the wind does.

Where does it come from?
From the clouds, the sky
Or perhaps the north, the south
The east and west
That's where the wind comes from.

Where does the wind go?
Through the trees, over seas
Under leaves, over hills
That's where the wind goes.

Richard Bombroffe (9) Highfields School

BELTON HOUSE

B is for bell on the front door so big and loud.
E is for the excited children who play in the playground.
L is for laughter that the children have dressing up.
T is for toilets that are so nice and clean.
O is for the orange trees in the orangery.
N is for the noisy kitchen where all the meals are prepared.

H is for the big big house where everyone comes to visit.
O is for the orchard where so many fruit trees grow.
U You will have a great time at Belton House.
S is for the station where little people go by train.
E is for the events like the horse trials and music concerts.

Jordan Lee (9) Highfields School

SCAMP AND TRAMP

There's a little dog called Scamp
that lives with a tramp.
And they live in a little old bin.
There's a rip at the tip and all the cold air rushes in
It's making them shiver and quiver and they wrap
up in an old lady's cloak.
They wear ragged jeans with holes in the knees
and dance around all night.
            Would you give them a bite to eat
or a copper or two as you pass by and stare
I would like to invite them in as long as they don't
live in my bin!

Merelina Monk (8) Highfields School

SUPER SPORT

One wonderful water-skier whizzing over waves.
Two terrible tennis players talking about a terrific time.
Three ball throwers thinking that they're tough.
Four fantastic footballers flicking footballs fast.
Five frightened figure skaters falling briskly forwards.
Six silly skiers sliding in the snow.
Seven stupendous swimmers strangely swishing sideways.
Eight angry anglers arguing on the Amazon.
Nine naughty netballers knocking nervous knees.
Ten trampolinists taking turns tossing, turning and tumbling.

Katy Morrison (9) Highfields School

TANTRUMS

When I am angry I slam the door,
Stamp my feet,
And shout 'No more!'
I scream and scream,
My face turns red,
I wont' be good and go to bed.

My sister teases,
My brother annoys,
He screams at me just like other boys.
I wish he would listen to what I say,
Instead of whining and running away.

When I am angry my brain goes mad,
It makes my family feel so sad,
I won't eat my dinner
I won't eat my tea,
Why won't they ever listen to me?

Harriet Applewhite (9) Highfields School

FEELING ANGRY

When I feel angry, I mean really angry, I shout and
slam doors and go to my room stamping and stamping.
I lie on my bed crying and do not come out.
When I decide to return I do not talk to the person that
has made me mad.
Oh no, here comes trouble, my brother. He always
annoys me . . .
>   'Ahhh!'
>   'Get out!'
>   'Go away!'

My brother teases me and is sometimes horrible to me.
It makes me feel like hitting him really hard.
I do hit him sometimes but he does not cry, which
makes me feel even madder. My face turns red with
raging temper.

Jessica Hand (9) Highfields School

SAD

Not being able to stay up at night,
people in wars destined to fight.
>   These things make me sad
Animals slaughtered for their meat,
burning trees killed by the heat.
>   These things make me mad.
Always having to share my sweets,
not being able to have treats.
>   These things make me sad.
Not being able to have a CD ROM,
someone in London killed by a bomb.
>   These things make me mad.

Kayleigh Hall (9) Highfields School

GOING ON HOLIDAY

I wake up and hear quiet noises outside.
I peep through the curtains.
I see mum and dad scurrying up and down.
It's dark when we set off.
I find it hard to get to sleep.

There are lights and noises of traffic.
Mum keeps saying 'Shut your eyes!'
When I wake up it's light!
In the distance is the sea.
I can smell the docks.

I feel excited when we draw up to the ferry.
It's very crowded and we search for somewhere to sit.
Later up on deck we can see France.
Our holiday has started.

Josh Rollin (9) Highfields School

I AM A PIANO

Once I was your pride and joy
unlike any other toy.
Once my silver strings plinked and rumbled
now my notes are mixed and jumbled.

Once my keys were black and white
You used to play me day and night.
Once my wood gleamed and shined
now your eyes for my notes are blind.

You used to play jazz, rock, classic, songs from the west
Beethoven, Mozart, Bach and some of the best.
Now my wood is scratched and dinted,
your fingers on my keys are printed.

Now my strings are old and rusty,
my music rack is old and dusty.
My music books are ripped and torn
I'm not as young as when I was born.

Soon I will be sold,
        because I'm battered, tattered and very worn.

Andrew Storey (9) John Blow Primary School

AT THE BEACH

The sea is rushing to the shore
crashing on the pebbly beach I
walk upon. In the rock pool I see
some crabs on the hard grey slabs.
The sea still pushing gushing
to the shore.

Carla Cockburn (10) Keyworth Primary & Nursery School

67

GHOST

The landing creaked with fear and fright
'Who's there?' he whispered in the dead of night
The handle turned and eyes were wide
The feelings changed let's curl up and hide.

The door opened and in he came
A peculiar face with a peculiar name
The boy just stared
And still he was scared, he was scared.

The ghost just stared back at the boy
As if all he was, was an imaginary toy
He looked away to find the light of day
But the night just seemed to stay, to stay.

Lindsey Frame (11) Keyworth Primary & Nursery School

ESCAPE

Hare, hare running free
How magic you seem to be
Running over the grassy ground
Hop by hop, bound by bound
Streaking past the leafy tree
Faster than a charging bee

Hare, hare are you free?
Are you lost because of me?
Men who kill by their will . . .
Why do you lie so still?

Hare, hare there you lie
How many more will die?

Vicky Fackrell (11) Keyworth Primary & Nursery School

JOYRIDERS

Jolly little Lucy goes out to play
With all her little playmates
To run about the hay.

First they have to cross the road to
get to the field
No adults to shield,
For these are seven year olds.

They stand at the edge of the road,
Then look to the left
And then to the right,
Not a car in sight.

Then it's time to cross right over,
They start off,
Still being very careful,
Then all of a sudden a screech of brakes,
Then suddenly *bang!*

Lucy, Jennifer, Paul and Dan all gone.
The car sped off at a great high speed,
Wonder how many more murders they've done.

Rachel Shields (11) Keyworth Primary & Nursery School

THE ROSE

The rose is many colours,
Tall on its own
And short in bunches,
It grows wildly on the walls.
The petals are soft as silk
with all the beauty,
The rose comes in summer,
But soon its petals will fall.

Emma Whitelam (9) Keyworth Primary & Nursery School

THE IRON MAN

Combing the beach
looking for himself,
Only one eye,
Only two hands,
Found the leg which he walks upon,
Found the head which he thinks with.
Only one ear to listen with
have to find the other ear,
maybe the sea has taken it
maybe the sea has lost it?

Kym Doughty (11) Keyworth Primary & Nursery School

OUTLAWS OF THE GLEN

Dark is the night,
High is the fire,
It torches the sky,
Rising higher and higher.

My courageous men draw around the warm
glow of the fire,
We close our eyes
And picture the victory.
We do despise
Prince John and his rebels.

We'll start destroying that castle from now
on.
Break down their defences one by one.
When that fortress is open wide, we'll go
right inside.

We're proud to wear our Lincoln Green.
Soon we shall hold our heads up high.
And King Richard will come riding home
from the war
And England will once more be ours!

Jane Archer (11) Keyworth Primary & Nursery School

LONELY

I feel locked up in a box,
waiting for someone
to lift the lid
and let the daylight drift in.

I am a candle blown out by the wind,
left in darkness
waiting for someone
to light me.

I am on my own,
love me someone
don't let me be lonely
a ship drowning in my unhappy tears,
lonely, no-one around,
deserted and alone.

Jane Boston (11) Keyworth Primary & Nursery School

ANNE FRANK - THE TRAGEDY

Locked up inside the secret annexe,
not to be heard our fears and panics.
Then tragedy knocked upon our door,
lifted our feet up from the floor.

Carried us off to Hitler's camps,
tortured us, burnt our faces with lamps,
sent us to work at the holocaust,
packed like sardines, pushed and forced.

Separated from family and friends,
told they are dead or they've gone round the bend.
Lost in despair, I'm sure I am dying,
too weak to scream,
too sad for crying.

Kate Allen (11) Keyworth Primary & Nursery School

CORAL PRINCESS

Here in the midst of a raging storm,
The icy blue waves foaming,
Crashing down around me,
The wind whipping up my long golden locks,
Then they fall,
Like a shower of gold.
The rain slashes into the iceberg on which I rest,
Tries to cut into the heart of the crystal dome,
No success meets the torment.
Thunder rolls above my head,
I hear cries of terror from sailors far away,
But no terror reaches my mind.
I cherish the thunder,
The music of one thousand stars,
A steady beating moon drum.
Lightning is a symbol of power to me,
It fills me with strength,
Every flash thrills me,
I feel as if nothing in the world could hurt me.
I, the coral princess,
Stand proud.

Sabina Mulloy (10) Keyworth Primary & Nursery School

DANGER

D anger means bad,
A thing that can kill you.
N ever go to danger.
G o to danger and die!
E lectricity is danger
R est in peace.

Matthew Beadsworth (8) Kimberley Primary School

ELECTRIC

E lectricity can kill
L et's not play near electricity
E lectricity can sometimes give you a shock
C an you see electricity?
T he voltage is high. It is 240 volts
R ead the signs on your TV
I am dangerous
C an you avoid electricity?

Alex Brown (9) Kimberley Primary School

DOLPHIN

D olphins live in the sea
O n the cliffs,
L ive seagulls.
P eople need the water.
H appy dolphins
I n the sea.
N ear and forever.

Amy Gathercole (8) Kimberley Primary School

BATTERY

B atteries are dangerous.
A nything that is electric can be dangerous.
T elephone wires can be dangerous.
T rains are dangerous.
E lectricity can be dangerous.
R inging bells do not use electricity.
Y ou can get killed by it.

Amy Fewster (8) Kimberley Primary School

LION

The lion with his golden
mane,
Strolls around his
territory.
He stops, he sees a rival,
After *his* mate!
He charges at him,
And wins . . .

That's my lion!

Hannah Ocheduszko (9) Kimberley Primary School

DOCTOR

Doctor doctor I feel funny
my head is spinning round
and round I keep falling
to the ground
I get up to get some toast
I think I saw a ghost
is it me is it true I think
I've got the flu
I think I want to go
to bed my head is feeling
really funny I think I need
a doctor honey
Doctor doctor I feel funny.

Kirsty Rowley (10) Kimberley Primary School

75

SCHOOL'S OUT

End of the day,
School's out.
Pencils gone,
Rubbers broke,
Paper gone,
Ink stain.
No children about,
Just a jumper.
When I go I feel so cool,
The old day has finished,
The new day's ahead.

Becky Duerden (9) Kimberley Primary School

ELECTRIC SHOCK

E lectricity kills.
L et's not go near it.
E lectricity kills.
C ats and other wild animals
T ry staying away from it!
R ing your friends, let them know.
I get done if I mess with it.
C ome with us and be safe.

S hocks can be fatal
H armful and painful.
O range light above your hospital bed.
C ourage,
K ills badly when you're alone.

Julie Rhodes (9) Kimberley Primary School

SCHOOL

School, school is really cool,
Maths,
English,
Take your pick,

But school dinners,
Are really sick.

PE on Monday,
Wednesday,
And Friday,
On Tuesday, we are going to
the library.

Jade Edis (9) Kimberley Primary School

DEEP DARK LAKE

Down in the
deep dark lake
lurked a deep
dark monster
everyone who
sees the monster shake
the animals quake and so do I
The monster rises
making gruffling snuffling noises
the animals fled
the humans shake
monster monster in the lake
go back down.

Robert Chambers (10) Kimberley Primary School

BATTERY

B atteries are electricity.
A battery is a kind of electricity;
T ravels up through the battery to make it light up.
T eachers teach us about electricity.
E lectricity runs through batteries.
R ed is on batteries.
Y ou use batteries on toys.

Rachael Messom (9) Kimberley Primary School

THE BIG YUKKY SPIDER

In a dark dark village
In a dark dark house
In a dark dark cellar
There's a dark dark staircase
Down the dark dark staircase
Into a dark dark room
In the dark dark room
There's a big yukky spider.

Gary Wood (10) Kimberley Primary School

MY DOG SAM

My dog Sam is my best friend,
He never argues with me,
He never fights with me,
We have lots of fun together,
He's the best dog in the world.

Ricky Duerden (8) Kimberley Primary School

JELLY

Jelly jelly,
Behind the door
Jelly jelly
On the floor
Jelly jelly
In my welly
Jelly jelly
In my belly
Jelly jelly
Eat more and more then you will go *pop.*

Jamie Rose (11) Kimberley Primary School

SPOTS

Spots, spots,
Everywhere they're on my face
but not in my hair
There's one spot on my nose
that grows and grows
My spots are like big red dots
they're on my belly
on my leg
The biggest one
as big as an egg
They're on my back
like blobs of Blue Tack
I've been off school
for three days now
They're getting on my nerves
What will I do to get rid of them
I really don't know how.

Matthew Watson (10) Kimberley Primary School

PICK ON ME

Pick on me
All you like
All day long I don't care

Pick on me because I have ginger hair
Pick on me because my dad's the mayor
Pick on me because I'm good at maths
Pick on me because I've got a funny laugh
Pick on me because my pen is blue
Pick on me because my friend is Sue
Pick on me because my house is red
Pick on me because I've got a big head
Pick on me because I am small
Pick on me because my friends are tall
Pick on me because my maths is right
Pick on me because it's darker at night
Pick on me because I like baby cubs
Pick on me because you like bugs
Pick on me because I've got a ring
Pick on me because you can't sing
Pick on me
All you like
All day long, *I don't care!*

Laura Matkin (11) Kimberley Primary School

MOON

The moon is a planet
The moon is weightless
The moon is a light
The moon is a neighbour
The moon is our friend.

Kieran Ahern (9) Kimberley Primary School

THE TAP

Drip drip what is that?
Is it raining outside?
It must be raining or a hole in the roof
Drip drip what is it?
Is it a burst pipe?
Or it could be the sticky bath tap.
Drip drip drip drip,
It is coming faster now
Just where is it coming from?
It is not raining so it is not the roof
It must be the sticky tap.

Charlotte Edwards (10) Kimberley Primary School

WATER

Sea water everywhere as calm as can be
Sea water splashing and sploshing against
the shining rocks
Sea water sparkling when the sunlight shines
When the sunlight shines it makes the
water glisten
Ripples of water running up the sandy beach
Sea water makes you cool in hot weather
Sea water tastes like salty water
Fish racing through the salty water
Sea water flying through the air with the
speed of a boat
Moonlight makes it calm and still and
alone.

Sarah Clarke (10) Kimberley Primary School

WHERE IS THE PLANET MARS?

Where is the planet Mars?
Is it full of buildings?
Is it full of cars?
Are there creatures with
horns on their heads?
How many of them could
be dead?
Red, yellow, orange and blue
They're not the same colour
as me or you.

Thomas Towlson (11) Kimberley Primary School

BLIND

Darkness darkness
Nothing but darkness,
Familiar sounds,
But not a picture,
Lovely sounds,
It's not fair, why?
Why did this happen to me?
Blind forever,
Blind forever,
Chris my friend,
Who was my friend
Now isn't my friend
Stupid boy,
He killed my eyes,
Thank you Chris,
Think,
Why?

Stephenie Crowe (11) Kimberley Primary School

WHO'S GOING TO WIN?

They're really all the same
but who's going to win that game?
It could be them,
It could be us,
Nobody knows,
Nobody should,
They'll put on their boots,
They'll kick the ball high,
And when the whistle toots
They'll play while the hours pass by.

Kayleigh Anderson (10) Kimberley Primary School

DARK DARK COUNTRY, LIGHT LIGHT ISLAND

In a dark dark country there is a dark dark town
In that dark dark town there's a dark dark street
In that dark dark street there's a dark bunch of houses
In one particular house there's a dark dark door
Through that dark door there is a room.

In that room there lies a bed
On that bed lies a puddle of *blood.*

That blood came from the sea witch and she lived
on a light light island.

On that light island there's a light light cottage.

In that light light cottage there is a
light light kitchen.
In that light kitchen there is a witch's bowl

In that bowl there is some blood, that blood
came from an undersea water monster. *He, he hee!*

Tony Johnson (10) Kimberley Primary School

THE RACE

The referee points his gun to the sky.
A drip of sweat falls down my face.
Then bang goes the gun, my legs spring
into action.
The wind swirls through my hair.
My legs are in agony as I pedal
up the hill.
I don't take a bit of notice of my thirst,
All that is in my head is
to win the race.
The track is hot and bumpy,
the sun scorches down on me.
But I carry on, one person is
in front of me.
I strain to catch up,
I overtake him and win the
race, everyone is cheering.

Robin Colley (9) Kinoulton Primary School

MY BICYCLE

I ride along the lanes and roads,
On my pink and purple bike.
I got my bike just yesterday,
And rode around under the stars.
It's a mountain bike with five gears,
I'm going for a picnic up in the hills.
I'll take crisps, ham, biscuits and apples,
To eat up in the hills.

Sarah Tyler (9) Kinoulton Primary School

84

RIDE TO THE ISLES

I went for a bike ride in Scotland,
Along the road to the Isles.
I pedalled so hard up the mountains,
I travelled for miles and miles.

Once, something leapt out of the woodland,
I nearly fell off my bike.
I froze to the spot as I watched the deer,
They were a staggering sight.

It was time to move on then,
The deer had all gone,
The wind whistled past me
Singing its song.

Descent to the loch side,
Shining and blue,
With its upside down pictures
Of mountains and snow.

I pedalled on to the harbour,
Spied Eigg, the volcanic rock.
I'd reached my destination.
Exhausted, I could stop.

Niki Popplewell (9) Kinoulton Primary School

THE BIKE

Bikes are big, bikes are small, bikes are fat, bikes are thin.
Children love to ride them and go for miles and miles.
When I go on a bike I feel like I blow away into a different world.
I like to ride my bike it is so fast,
When I ride my bike I go up, down, up, down, up and down.

Shane Bullivant (9) Kinoulton Primary School

BICYCLES

Bicycles, bicycle tyres and wheels,
I like the ones that look like seals,
Lots of saddles and lots of chains,
I made a toy bike out of canes,
Bikes are big, bikes are small,
Some are tiny some are tall,
My bike is nice,
My bike is small,
My bike is crazy,
And that's not all,
My bike can go fast,
My bike can go slow,
And my bike is called Mrs *Big Toe.*

Natalie Tomany (10) Kinoulton Primary School

THE SOUNDS OF WAR

The sound of bombs dropping down to
the ground.
The sound of war, the sound of the
planes falling down to the ground.
The sound of the tanks' engines rumbling
across the ground.
The sound of the bombs exploding on the
ground.
The sound of explosions filling the
air. Planes swerving through the
air. Sirens calling as the day is
dawning and people running.

Joe Wilkins (8) Kinoulton Primary School

ALL ABOUT BIKES

Bikes are fast, bikes are slow.
Bikes are skidding through the snow
Bikes are colourful, bikes
      can be big.
Bikes can do skids.

Bikes are cool!

Joanne Pinks (9) Kinoulton Primary School

SONG OF WAR

The song is long
In war when they sing
The soldiers sing when they are
Marching.
Sound of bombs dropping
Down down down, dropping on, on
The ground. Then a bomb drops down
Bang, bang, bang!

Rachael Hall (8) Kinoulton Primary School

THE COLOURS OF WAR

Green, brown and black
Are the colours of war.
These are the clothes that soldiers wore
When they went ashore
To get to the other side
Where lots of people have died.
Where guns have fired.

Jacob Sanderson (7) Kinoulton Primary School

COLOURS OF WAR

The colours of war
Are black and brown.
Black is the bomb
Going down down down.
The air raid shelter is grey,
The tank is black and green
Going on its way.
The house is brown going down down down,
By the bomb, bomb, bomb.

Felicity Price (8) Kinoulton Primary School

THE FEELINGS OF WAR

When I was in the war I felt sad,
And some soldiers felt mad.
Then the Germans threw a bomb.
And I started to sing a song.
I sang a song so that I wouldn't be scared,
Then the English people got prepared,
Then I saw a Spitfire in the sky,
And I saw someone who was about to die.

Jennifer Salt (8) Kinoulton Primary School

THE SOUND OF WAR

Bombs are dropping everywhere
Run run to the bomb shelter.
Get the gas masks on
Quickly. Plane sounds
Sounds everywhere.
Homes smashed. Bricks
Everywhere. Bombs stopped
And the planes were gone
and it was peace.

Stuart Neaves (8) Kinoulton Primary School

PRISONER

Dark curtains of gloom and hate hanging
over lands of bitterness and destruction.

Cages of wailing lost souls imprisoned behind
iron bars of hate.

Dead feelings locked behind windows of
depression.

Beings of sadness whining like howling dogs.
Droplets of death dripping all around me.
I hate this world.

Emma Orton (10) Linby cum Papplewick Primary School

TRAPPED

Trapped inside a wall of blackness,
Ghosts come out to haunt me,
Shadows behind my curtain,
Telling me my future like a crystal ball,
People asking me questions,
Screaming them out,
Grabbing on to my brain,
Covering it in a curtain of doom.

Matthew Turner (10) Linby cum Papplewick Primary School

SEA

The waves lapping on the shore
Glistening in the sun;
The waves started crashing against the rock,
While the seal was basking in the sun,
Listening to the calls of the seagulls.
Far away in the distance
Is a boat beating against the horn.
The sea is peaceful,
Maybe I should go there.

Cassie Whitehead (11) Linby cum Papplewick Primary School

SUN

The sun is bright,
the sky is blue,
the clouds are white as snow.
The grass is green,
and the trees are brown.

Steven Sheppard (9) Linby cum Papplewick Primary School

NUCLEAR WAR

I see a missile landing on a terror warped
world, causing total carnage and fear.

I see them all running away from death,
trying to save their lives and others.

I see the bombers using chemical warfare,
eliminating everyone causing total
genocide.

And all because of one tiny thing.

William Burnett (9) Linby cum Papplewick Primary School

LION

Golden fur smooth and soft,
Blends in with his fiery gold mane,
His slender healthy body and his green glinting eyes,
Have an enigmatic look,
Teeth like icicles curved sharp and strong.
Close like a cage around his pink lolling tongue,
He laps up water then holds his head high,
Like a hinge,
Tail swinging like a pendulum,
His opulent look stately and proud.

Hannah Page (10) Linby cum Papplewick Primary School

PRACTICE UNTIL YOU GET IT RIGHT

Sit down, practice your singing
practice after school
practice in playtimes
just practice until you get it right
practice in shops
practice it in front of your pet
practice until you get it right
practice it in the wardrobe
practice it when eating
practice until you get it right
practice it in the bath
practice it in the zoo
practice until you get it right
practice on a journey
practice under water
practice until you get it right
Practice.

Kim Ward (9) Linby cum Papplewick Primary School

GHOST

Squeak as the door opens in the darkness of hell,
A clear figure floats through the air of the black sheet
of night,
A baby's scream in the background,
As the ghost crawls on the quilt,
The baby stops,
A dog bark takes over.

Lee March (10) Linby cum Papplewick Primary School

THE DREAM

I was drifting away to a land
  of flowers and trees until
I fall on the floor and I go through a
  door of horror. I saw a ghost,
some were thin, some were fat.
Some tripped up on my teddy bear's hat,
The room was dark and then all of a
sudden a great ball of light struck my eyes
and it was just the morning sun gleaming into my eyes.

Charlotte Atkin (9) Linby cum Papplewick Primary School

A FREE TIGER

Orange striped tiger,
camouflaged in the shadow.
The tiger loves wildebeest,
for the tiger it's a real feast.
The majestic hunter pounces,
with a baby deer on the animal's claw,
he goes to his lair to eat,
but soon he will be looking for more.

The animal is strong and sleek,
he runs and runs with pattering feet.
The animal sees antelope walking around,
I bet the tiger is thinking look what
I've found.
He takes a wildebeest to the floor,
and he will be back another day I'm sure.

Patrick Dandy (10) Lowes Wong Junior School

JUNGLE ANIMALS

Monkeys leap from tree to tree
Little faces smile at me.
Kissing, kicking, having fun.
Young ones, old ones, snooze in the sun.

Snakes slither along the ground,
Up the trees without a sound.
A little bird tries to fly away,
He grabs her legs in his mouth,
But when he sees her little blue eggs
He changes his mind
And the little bird leaves him behind.

Claire Fletcher (9) Lowes Wong Junior School

SEASONS

Autumn, winter, summer, spring,
Some people wear a season ring.
If I wore one I would be very glad,
Never again would I be sad.

Summer can be very hot,
That's why I like it quite a lot.
I'm in a better mood in spring,
I sometimes even like to sing.

Autumn can be very mild,
I sometimes feel like a baby child.
Winter can be very cold,
People don't like it, I am told.

Rebecca Peacock (9) Lowes Wong Junior School

JENNY THE DOLL

Squashed in the attic.
Gloomy, dark and creepy.
I once was happy.
Now I'm sad.
I'm forgotten and neglected.
Dirty, broken, chipped and faded.
My lace is torn and parts are missing.
There are rats scurrying below me
in the shadows.
I'm an old doll thrown in the attic.
One hundred years ago I was treated
like a child.
I was wanted.
I was cherished by my owner
She sat me on a shelf
Now I'm in the attic
It's damp and sticky.
And it seems like the end of me.

Harriet Danby (8) Lowes Wong Junior School

IMAGINE

Imagine the war going on and on,
Imagine the cannon smoke blocking out the sun.
Imagine not being able to think,
Imagine not being able to have a drink.

Why do I wish this war would start?
My heart beats getting really fast.
I've never been to war before,
Blood and guts, mess and gore!

Emily Goodwin (10) Lowes Wong Junior School

THE POND

Ducks are dabbling in the pond
their heads are under water
to catch their lunch before too late
to feed their son and daughter

Fish are swimming round and round
their mouths are open wide
they feed on weed and water mites
that disappear inside

The water boatman twists and dives
beneath the fishes fin
the water skater skims and slides
across the surface skin

I like to sit beside the pond
it's peaceful and it's quiet
until the noisy geese arrive
and always start a riot.

Lucy Poyzer (9) Lowes Wong Junior School

HELICOPTER

Buzzing humming like a bee.
Coming closer starting to roar,
Floating, flying like a bird,
It's so windy, like a storm.
The loudest noise I've ever heard,
Flying swiftly, closer still,
Landing softly.
Engines off, pilots out,
A cheer goes up.
That was great!

Jonathan Curtis-Bell (9) Lowes Wong Junior School

96

WEIRD DREAMS!

As I lie down against the rickety wall; I realise I have
to fight and survive against the Roundheads. I must
fight for my King and country. I drift in and out of
sleep. In my mind I hear the clashing of swords and the
colossal bang of muskets.

I am given bread and water. I have 20 hours to
rest and I know I must use them well. I think forward
to the great battle. The early morning sun shatters
my thoughts. I yawn and stretch. And I hear a voice. 'You
soldier, don't you know you have a battle to fight.' I say
a quick prayer and am called to arms.

Martin Stretch (10) Lowes Wong Junior School

WHAT'LL HAPPEN

I'm tired and weary from the
Miles and miles I've travelled to get to Maplefield,
I'm hungry, excited, worried and sad,
What'll happen to me over the next hours?

The woman came to feed me bread
With cheese and butter in the basket,
I rested my head against the trunk of a tree.
At once I got a thought in my head.

I started dreaming
I heard screaming and shouting,
Blood and gore
Pain and despair,
Could I stand the civil war?

Rachel Watts (10) Lowes Wong Junior School

97

THE NIGHT BEFORE THE WAR

There was some men starving as
I rush to give them bread and milk.
As I go on and on I can hear their cries
As I walk by.

I think to myself some of these men
Will be dead on the field of Edge Hill.
I cried as I went back to my mum
For more bread and milk.

Then a shout came from the soldier.
They all stood up and marched off.
When they came back they were all tired
They will never be fit and well for tomorrow
I thought.

Catherine Frazer (10) Lowes Wong Junior School

THE NIGHT BEFORE I WENT TO WAR

I'm staying at Edgehill,
Just behind a dusty mill.
The ladies came with food in baskets,
As I was shining my new musket.
I've never used a pike before,
In fact I've never been to war.
My thoughts now are really milling,
Blood and gore, injuries, killing.
Taking a bite out of my bread,
As more thoughts run into my head.
Please God make us victorious,
And if we are, make it glorious.

Helen Rajan (10) Lowes Wong Junior School

NIGHT BEFORE DREADED DAY

It had been a weary day.
And I lay my tired head down on the rough bark of the old oak
My restless body turning over and over again on the dry grass,
My mood frightened, hungry, worried.

I hear voices flowing through my confused head,
Screaming, shouting, banging,
My heart beating faster, faster, faster.
As my beating heart beats faster my mind starts panicking.

The noise is taking over me,
I feel weak.
I fall into a deep sleep,
I dream of being defeated.

The muskets banging in my ear,
The horrible voice of people dying.
And the cry of mothers and children,
As they nurse their beloved one's wounds.

Victoria Farren (10) Lowes Wong Junior School

LIZARDS

Waiting for its prey,
Hoping for something each day.
When it comes
He starts to run
Then swallows it up hooray.

I am small and camouflaged,
With a long long tongue,
licking up his dinner with,
a happy song.

Jack Cottam (10) Lowes Wong Junior School

99

I'D HATE IT TO BE ME

Cooking a chicken
For the soldiers' tea,
The leader shouting at a man,
I'd hate it to be me.
All we want is
        Victory.

Someone's crying
under a tree,
I'd hate it to be me.
A sword in his hand
and a musket under his arm.
If he's careful
He'll come to no harm.

Cooking a chicken
For the soldiers' tea,
The leader shouting at a man,
I'd hate it to be me.
Will we get our
        Victory?

Joanna Ford (10) Lowes Wong Junior School

THE WATERFALL

Gurgling and gushing,
Racing and rushing,
Noisily calling,
Hurriedly falling,
Twisting and twirling,
Bubbling and swirling.

Claire Undy (9) Lowes Wong Junior School

WILL I STAND

I shake with cold
Will I stand
I lay against my canon.
I am a gun captain of 15 years
A dragoon bugler talks to me.
We lean against his horse,
He shares his bread with me.

I tell my fears to my friend
He tells me to keep my head and I'll
Be all right.
I drift to sleep with thoughts of fear,
Will I stand will I run
Will I hear the sound of the guns
I hear sounds of shouting sounds of crying

Will I stand
It is morning now,
My fear is gone
I hope I will survive.

Christopher Lowe (10) Lowes Wong Junior School

THE NIGHT BEFORE THE BATTLE

I have had a long day's journey. I try
to rest but after half an hour I drifted off.

I dreamt of all the blood and gore that
awaited me. Would I die or would I live?

A little glint of sunlight that shone
through the trees woke me up. I ran to
my ranks.

Ben Cowley (9) Lowes Wong Junior School

THE TIGER

In the darkness
The tiger prowls
Hunting for its prey.
It comes across
A deer and lies down
Ready to pounce.
Then the tiger jumps.
The deer tries to run
But it has no chance
Against the tiger
After its meal the
Tiger lies down to
Sleep.

Alice Moore (10) Lowes Wong Junior School

THE LEOPARD

The leopard is a nimble creature,
Which has a fast observing and a graceful feature.
He comes out at day hurriedly looking for his
prey.
As quick as light the leopard is in the air,
Leaping for the poor mouse.
In one big gulp the mouse is gone
The leopard is slow.
As he lingers on.
The night has come the leopard is back
He's come for more in one big batch.
He's got some food but it's not much.
He'll get some more,
Very soon I'm sure.

Alison Wright (10) Lowes Wong Junior School

RED FOX

Red fox,
Red fox,
Where are you?

I crept out into the garden,
Shivering in the cold.

Looking in the hedge and in the tree
house bare.

But where was the fox?

There was a hole,
full with grass and twigs.

There was the fox with babies
to hold.

They were shivering in the cold.
I brought them in our house to
hold.

Chloe Coops (9) Lowes Wong Junior School

BATS

In the dark in the middle of the night there is
a black bat,
Screeching for its tea,
Sees a moth goes into the shadow,
Then flies out and grabs the moth,
And hangs on a tree and eats it.

Nicholas Sharp (10) Lowes Wong Junior School

THE DRAGON

Fire spurts out, from the dragon's nose,
Sets alight all things in range!
Men all run and women all scream,
As their houses are burnt down to smithereens!
Her wings beat up and down gracefully,
Till she's one hundred feet up and climbing still.
A piercing shriek fills the skies.
Almost blinding the ears of all things in the air,
But the dragon's deeds are not over yet
For she swooped down and grabbed an unexpecting boy!
The boy was killed by the dragon's claws,
As they took off almost straight up
Dragon goes to a hide in a mountain
Rambles through the passage
And drops the boy in a pile of meat
Then she attends to three dragon eggs.
Three more eggs mean three more murderous dragons
Three times the terror and three times the fright.

Aaron Oliver-Taylor (10) Lowes Wong Junior School

GUESS WHO

I'm a bit of a weird animal.
Some people think of me as a mermaid.
I'm nearly extinct.
I don't live in a sink but I do live
in water.
I'm fat and ugly.
I'm more likely to be seen in America
    Yes it's me the ...
      Manatee.

Holliegh Gallon (10) Lowes Wong Junior School

THE NIGHT BEFORE THE BATTLE

I'm an ordinary soldier
Just an age ten
If I survive I will never come again

I just have the thoughts of war
I had to walk all the way
Now my legs are sore

I had 13 hours of training
It was so very hard
It nearly did my brain in

As I listen to the sounds of crying
I polish my musket
All I do is sighing

As I lay against a tree
Horrid images
Forever haunt me

I feel my eyes beckoned me
to go to sleep
But it's only for a second you see

I hear my dear brother has died
If I die God will be my guide.

Lauren Hotchkiss (10) Lowes Wong Junior School

THE MIGHTY LION

On the last African plains
The mighty lion comes out to hunt.
He stealthily creeps looking for prey
And suddenly vanishes from view.
A cold uncertainty feeling strikes
some Gazelle.

The kill came quiet and sudden,
The Gazelle didn't know it happened.
They stood there scared day and night,
Too scared to even move.
They waited for the lion to make his
move,

The move that had already been,
They never moved again,
Till the next time,
That is.

Richard Hill (10) Lowes Wong Junior School

THE AMERICAN BULL FROG

In the dark gloomy pool.
The fish are swimming round.
Then suddenly a dark shape
Comes and eats them one by one
First you see the frog-spawn
swaying in the current.
Then half are gone.
A frog is swimming
it swims to the corner
Then it's gone.
It's the American Bull Frog.

James Kirkham (10) Lowes Wong Junior School

I DON'T KNOW MUCH ABOUT THE ZEBRA

I don't know much about the zebra,
It's a black-and-white striped horse-type creature.
Where does it live?

Italy, New Jersey, Australia, York?
Maybe Ireland, addressed through the post as *Cork.?*
I don't know much about the zebra -
What does it eat?
Pizzas with extra cheese,
Mice in the deep freeze,
Or nice green leaves from the tall green trees?
I don't know much about the zebra,
It's a black-and-white striped horse-type creature.

Bel Kraay (10) Lowes Wong Junior School

THE MYSTERIOUS ZEBRA!

The zebra is mysterious,
With its wonderful striped coat,
He's totally black and white,
And similar to a horse,
But very much prettier.
I'd love to meet a zebra,
While travelling through Africa,
And get to rub its beautiful coat,
To have a ride upon his back,
And make good friends with it,
But I have one small problem,
It wouldn't understand me!

Zoë Ellis (10) Lowes Wong Junior School

SEALS IN THE SEA

Down in the sea at the bottom of the ocean
Lots of seals live.
They play and scream
Squeal and shout
They catch their fish
And eat and eat them up.
Fast as fast can be.
They fight and bite
And sometimes very badly.
They lie on the rocks by
The bay and get their sun tan
Day by day.
The thing I care about most
Is the seals being hurt by the fishermen.
They kill them and eat them up for the supper.
They shoot them and poach them,
The horrid horrid men.

Nicola Brown (10) Lowes Wong Junior School

SPACE JOURNEYS

Clattering crunch, crunch, like crisp packets
The dark blue sky with sparkling stars,
With the blackness tightening around me,
Silent is what space is,
The planets twirling around me, I feel like the sun, boiling with anger.
On the moon my light goes,
But then my journey's over
I'll miss it
I'll miss it forever.

Punam Bhalla (10) Lowes Wong Junior School

STALKER

A beautiful mustardy brown body covered
with dark ink black stripes
He sees a graceful red deer
He starts stalking like a big cat
The strong long legs start up like a tractor
Off he goes
As fast as light
racing through the mysterious jungle
The shivering animals stagger to safety
hearts beating as fast as drums
then silence
The stalker strikes again.

Bryony Holt (10) Lowes Wong Junior School

SPACE

As black as a tom cat in the dark.
Multi coloured planets sparkling in the night.
Blackness falls.
All I hear is whooshing sounds as shooting stars
whizz by.
Then it becomes silent as death in a graveyard.
Boom! We land on the moon.
I look around . . . nothing. Absolutely nothing.
Then I hear a squelching sound,
like mud falling to the ground.
I feel a stab of fear catch my throat.
I spin around and see something.
A thousand thoughts whirled around my mind.
Could they be UFOs or could they be aliens?
But then I realised it was just the oil dripping
from it.

Joshua J M Box (9) Lowes Wong Junior School

A TIGER

A tiger
is not just a cat
sitting on a mat.
Its massive pounce
doesn't just hurt an ounce.
When it does its exciting tricks
the time just ticks.
It really is very fast.
It just races past.
Sometimes wrong
but very strong.
Speeding through the tropical jungle
in a massive bungle.
Its incredible speed
helps it do its deed.
As long as a train
With a big hairy mane.
Its pace
Always wins the race.

Ben Tanner (9) Lowes Wong Junior School

THE INTRUDER

The spiky spiny creature
Wanders round the grassden
And itches through the hedge
And rolls over the colourbed
Then goes through the miaow-flap
Next he scrumbles up the bumpy hill
And turns right-ear and then again
He ploddles along the furway
And turns left paw into a room
He sees a bouncy bed and crawls in!

In the light-time the spiker
Comes out and rolls out of the room
And down the dumpy hill. Oh no!
A miaow! It hisses and lashes at the animal
The animal rolls into a ball and charges!
Miiaaoowww! The cat gasps for breath.
The animal portles back across the colourbed.
He walks to his hole in the grassden.

Mark Pearce (9) Lowes Wong Junior School

THE ACROBAT

Spider scurrying across his web.
Twisting twirling round my head,
There he is balancing on one leg.
How he loves to hang upside down.
There he is spinning his beautiful silver web.
As he dances along on his tiny matchstick
legs.
He looks like a tiny ballerina.
What a lovely sight he is,
The spider steadily balancing on his silver
tightrope.
Isn't he beautiful the way he does it?
He's so much like an acrobat.
There he is hanging upside down.
He's just so clever,
His body looks like a beautiful Easter egg,
There's his silvery silky web.
How pretty it is,
There he is twisting his body round his
silken thread like an acrobat but experienced.

Aimee Cottam (8) Lowes Wong Junior School

TIGER

The most feared animal in the jungle raises its head.
It leans forward,
Sniffing the pure, clean air.
A young deer comes into its sight,
The agile body stiffens.
Quietly it rises,
The formidable animal aims,
A sleek, swift blur charges,
Like a cork popping out of a bottle.
Wind rushes,
Orange and black merge together.
Sharp, steel, scissor-like claws unsheathe,
Then it pounces.
Strong jaws slam,
Dagger-like fangs tear and cut skin.
The deer is dead.
The solitary animal drags its prey into the bushes.
All that is left to show of the graceful tiger's attack is a
Few footprints in the dusty ground.

Helen Stark (10) Lowes Wong Junior School

THE WIND

I am a gentle breeze.
I blow paper around the street,
I hum and sing each day.
I blow rubbish.
I tiptoe everywhere.
I hum peacefully.
I am a calm and gentle breeze.
I make a peaceful humming noise.
I am the wind.

I am a gale.
I am a robber who snatches your hat and scarf.
I turn umbrellas inside out.
I chase people around
I push people over.
I whistle with my fingers
I kick the withered leaves.
I thump the branches with my hand.
I am a gale.

Lucy Hetherington (8) Lowes Wong Junior School

TIGERS

The tiger is a mighty creature
Strong and hypnotic
King of the Jungle
As fast as the blink of an eye
So why don't we
Let them be free
Trapped behind steel bars
Instead of in the jungle
They're near all the cars
Near all the people
Near all the noise
Away from their family
It's not fair
They won't learn how to hunt
They will have to be fed
And if we don't be careful
They will soon all be dead.

Natalie Wright (10) Lowes Wong Junior School

SPACE-EXPLORING THE UNEXPLORED

Pitch black skies.
Bright red fires.
Clear blue seas.
Pure green lands.
Shiny silver stars.
Sleek white rockets.
Burning coloured rings around planets.
Silent, gloomy, is the wide outdoors.
But then quiet music is coming from the stars.
Sounds like violins.
A whole orchestra.
Slowly the music dies down.
But the experience lives on.

Edward Hillier (10) Lowes Wong Junior School

THE KING OF THE JUNGLE

The King of the Jungle
Standing high
Glossy fur
Tigers.
The King of the Jungle
Running with thought
Stalking its prey
Graceful leaps
Tigers.
The King of the Jungle
Smooth strides
As quiet as an ant
Eating meat
Covered with blood
Tigers.

Emily Perry (10) Lowes Wong Junior School

THE LAMENT OF THE LEAD SOLDIER

In the attic
I sit, a little lead soldier,
It was gloomy,
It was cold,
The only survivor of many battles,
forgotten and neglected
'I was a disgrace'
to my regiment,
My uniform was ruined and
the buttons had fallen off,
my boots were lost.
It was dusty.
In the attic there were other toys.
I remembered when I was played with
when I was new and when the children
laughed.

Toby Robinson (8) Lowes Wong Junior School

THE ACROBAT

Webs like silver doilies with acrobatic
spiders swinging across. The silver web
shines like a diamond.

I wonder how the spider does it. The spider
sways across its web like an acrobat
on a trapeze. The web is so shiny it's
like a shooting star. Just think
how lovely it would be if you could
dance on silk. I bet an acrobatic spider
can catch a dozen flies a day
in its shining web!

David Proctor (8) Lowes Wong Junior School

115

THE WIND

I am a gentle breeze.
I rustle the leaves.
And make ripples in the grass so that it almost looks as if
it is changing colours.
I whisper lullabies to people who are lonely.
I brush your face with my gentle fingers.
And stroke your hair.
I am calm and relaxing.
I make the grass shiver
As I sing my haunting song.

I am a violent gale.
I uproot trees and damage buildings.
I snatch up flowers and shatter windows.
I cause chaos and destruction.
I am a robber.
A thief.
I steal hats and gloves.
I am bossy and cruel.
I am spiteful and mischievous
I tug and steal
I take tiles off roofs and bend trees.

I break big branches off the trees
and spit them out
I toss rubbish about
and trap it in wire netting
almost like fish in a net.
I push and tug
I am a bully.

Leanne Scothern (8) Lowes Wong Junior School

TIGER

A shiny orange body with pitch black stripes.
Gleaming in the evening sunset.
Ready to pounce violently on that poor lonely zebra.
Hypnotic eyes,
Fluidly leaping from tree to tree
Stalking a baby antelope.
Synchronising the leaps from branch to branch
As fast as the crack of a nut.
Speeding through the shadowy jungle
planning tactics skilfully
like a clan of military officers
walking back to the pack
as slow as the healing of the wound.

Jake Hall (10) Lowes Wong Junior School

THE LIONESS!

She roams around robust and strong,
Her body's sleek and oh so long,
Her powerful tail swishes and sways,
The annoying little pests away,

She'd wander through the undergrowth,
Looking for a tasty roast,
Just waiting there to be eaten,
She's surely going to have a feasting,
Her cubs will enjoy that meal for sure,
They will definitely ask for more,

But many people would prefer,
A tabby cat compared to her.

Paul Thompson & Ben Saunders (11) Lowes Wong Junior School

117

CAPTIVITY

Tigers,
Strong, fast,
Surprising.
Treated like they don't have feelings by the wrong people.
Why are we so cruel?
Captured, bribed to do tricks,
Used for people's entertainment.
They can't get their own back with their teeth as sharp as blades
If they do they get punished for it.
Escape is impossible.
Trapped in cold iron cages.
Taken away from their habits,
Their home,
Their family.
Under control by the humans
Forced to be given lifeless food.
But they need to hunt
Or they will slowly fade away.
Snatched out of nature.
They used to be feared
Now they're 'cute' or 'cuddly'
Surely now they know what hell is like.

Ben Griffiths (10) Lowes Wong Junior School

A PUZZLE POEM

I rampage round my field,
I'm difficult to catch,
I was a regular dish for some
but disease did I catch.

My horns generally scare people!
My size is very *big*.
The noise I make is deafening.
I got stuck between the gate posts,
A big roar comes towards me,
I'm feeling scared.
I'm a nice fellow really
But soon I'll be dead.

Mark Rainbow (10) Lowes Wong Junior School

YOU'RE A MIRACLE

You're a perfect creature
Sealed safely in a womb,
Completely unknown
Who will you be?
How will you smile?
What will make you cry?
Innocent and new,
You're pure and helpless
What treats you have in store.
You've never heard the sea crashing on the rocks,
Nor smelled the flowers in spring.
You've never felt the sun shining on your face,
Nor seen your mum's soft smile.
You're silent,
You're patient,
You're waiting,
For the door of life to open.

Hannah Magor (11) Lowes Wong Junior School

TIGERS

Tigers.
Big cats with glistening eyes like tiny lamps.
Slinking, crawling along gracefully
Stalking its helpless prey.
Camouflaged by trees and shrubs in the dense
jungle.
Pouncing,
Jaws wide, teeth out.
Bringing down a zebra with razor-sharp claws.
Cutting into the flesh of its victim.
Blood-stained mouth back to its den.
Tigers.

Thomas Moor (10) Lowes Wong Junior School

TIGERS!

Big tigers, little tigers, strong tigers, weak tigers, fast tigers,
slow tigers, thin tigers, fat tigers,
are all looking for their prey,
So please don't kill all the tigers because they are here to stay.
Some are locked up in zoos,
Some are free to run,
But some of them are whipped and kicked in a circus just for fun.
All tigers should be free to live their jungle life,
To run and run,
And catch their deer,
To live like tigers should,
So please don't kill all the tigers because they are here for good.

Kate McCallum (10) Lowes Wong Junior School

TRAPPED IN JAIL

Trapped in here all alone.
Nothing to pounce on
Nothing at all.
Nothing to growl at
Nothing to fight,
Nothing to scare.
With my shining silver glowing swords.
My tail is as long as a snake.

Bhavni Patel (10) Lowes Wong Junior School

I'M AFRAID OF THE DARK

I'm afraid of the dark,
The ghostly shadows in people's gardens.
I'm afraid of the dark.
The ghostly shadows that jump out from the
corners of my room.
I'm afraid of the dark.
There's no sound now.
But then creaking footsteps
Mounting the stairs,
I'm afraid of the dark.
I think I can hear some creepy gurgling
or is it the drain pipes?
I'm afraid of the dark.
I think I can see something lurking
behind my window.
I'm afraid of the dark.

Daniel Huson (8) Lowes Wong Junior School

121

THE ACROBAT

There is the spider hanging upside down, spinning
very fast.
He makes his web with threads of silk and then he has his
tea.
He scuttles across the floor to make someone scream.
Then the spider dangles upside down.
He swings from thread to thread.
The spider does a somersault on his web.

Grace Moore (8) Lowes Wong Junior School

CAPTURE

Tiger comes nearer to its prey.
Its eyes are glaring, staring
Full of enchantment.
Orange coat like fire, ready to pounce
Suddenly it stumbles into a trap
Men come out from nowhere
A cage comes down like hell on a string
The speedy hunter trapped like a mouse
The tiger is loaded on to a truck as though its whole life is one big joke
The truck drives away from its home,
From its place
No-one knows
It is looking death in the face.

Rebecca Rennison (10) Lowes Wong Junior School

DEATH BECOMES HIM

Great white shark,
They attack at dark,
Surfer falls in the water,
The shark caught him,
Another shark comes,
They feast on this rare delicacy,
Will he survive?
They looked in the day and in the dark,
But they never found him or the shark!

Christopher Naisbitt (11) Lowes Wong Junior School

SPACE

Aliens like green bananas
As thin as a stick
Klick klick klong klong
As they sleep with a zong.

UFOs screeching like a bird
Going through black holes
Which are as black as crows' feathers.

Boulders flying at our shuttle
Black as danger
I may be dodging, diving, swerving and curving.

Emily Evans (10) Lowes Wong Junior School

OUTER SPACE

UFOs buzzing like busy bumble bees in
the glimmering night sky.
Inky black sky turns bloody red then butter yellow
The endless darkness is broken.
Sizzly sun burns down on earth.
Planets twirling all around me.
A rocket shoots up
The satellite swirls around.
My space feeling is gone.

Kerri Clay (9) Lowes Wong Junior School

THE PLAINS OF AFRICA

In the beautiful plains of Africa
There is a breath-taking sight.
With brown tree stumps.
Hippos as grey as an old battered
church.
The water is like a white burning
fire.
It's a beautiful sight.
It makes me feel so free.

Emma Randle (10) Lynncroft Primary School

AFRICAN LADY AFRICAN CHILD

A frican lady African child

F inding a well of water

R each for the rope reach for the
bucket reach for your child as well.

I n the blazing hot sun she
carries the water.

C hasing her camel back home.

A frican lady African child back
home safe and sound.

Kim Read (11) Lynncroft Primary School

AFRICA

A frica's hot golden sand
F lying across the
R emaining dry desert
I n boiling temperatures,
C amels roam with bright jewellery
A nd riches beyond your wildest dreams . . .
follow the stars nomads say but you just
roam on
        and
           on
             and
               on . . .

Lindy Deaton (11) Lynncroft Primary School

THE CAMEL

The blistering sun is beating down on my
burning back.
Searching for water all day.
My weary feet sinking into the sand.
No energy left to walk another step.
A speeding sandstorm is on the way.
So I close my eyes, nose and mouth.
I sense where I'm going,
The desert is dry and dusty.
The wind is pounding in my face.

Peter Lowery (11) Lynncroft Primary School

THE STARS

The stars stars are so sparkly
and bright.

The stars stars are so very
silvery bright.

The stars stars are so
yellow bright.

The shooting stars travel so
quickly and bright,
and give us, oh such light!

Nigel Li (11) Manvers Junior School

TRAPPED

We are trapped.
Trapped forever.
Trapped in a cage.
Trapped forever.
I've got nowhere to stroll,
Trapped forever.
I hope we get free
But we are
Trapped forever!

Bryan Duncan (11) Manvers Junior School

THE MOON

The moon is rough,
The moon is tough,
With large and small craters.

The moon is rough,
The moon is tough,
With acres and acres of dust.

The moon is rough,
The moon is tough,
With nothing there but dirt.

The moon is rough,
The moon is tough,
The satellite of Earth.

The moon is rough,
The moon is tough,
Shining in the night.

Robin Stevenson (10) Manvers Junior School

BLOODY SPORT

A normal day, a normal life of a fox,
But then . . .
The deadly sound of a hunter's horn,
now it's a matter of life and death.
So you run!
Run as fast as your little legs can carry you!
The earthquaking sound of hooves behind you,
stops your pounding little heart.
The humans, it seems,
want the blood and life of me . . .
For a sport!
The blood thirsty hounds are on me, nearly!
I have to stop but if I do,
the hounds will turn me, into one billion jigsaw pieces,
that cannot be put back together.
An innocent life will be taken,
because man enjoys ripping animals' lives apart.
　　　It's a bloody sport!

Robert Perry (11) Manvers Junior School

WE WERE FREE . . .

We're free, we shake the earth with our
heavy grey feet
But the silence is broken by a soft whisper
There's a hunter a-foot!
Run lads run!
But there's the mighty river
We cannot go on!
When I wake up I'm in a dark cage
all alone . . . all alone . . .

Angie Mason (10) Manvers Junior School

128

THE TIGER IN A CAGE

The tiger looks up to a dream.
Beyond those iron bars,
The lush green grass with antelope to hunt,
Is beyond those iron bars,
The tiger paces up and down,
Dreaming, dreaming, dreaming.

Behind those iron bars is a tiger!
Just artificial grass,
With no food to hunt,
He is inside what seems a big dungeon.
No corners to lurk around,
No places to hide.

Up comes a human.
The tiger jumps up,
Thinking he will have a key,
To let him free.
But in despair he hears a child laugh,
'Daddy, can I feed the tiger?'
'No he's far too dangerous.'
The tiger lies down in a heap of artificial grass,
The zoo keeper comes up, with some steak,
The tiger eats it whilst dreaming
of eating an antelope,
Dreaming, dreaming, dreaming.

Alex Farran (11) Manvers Junior School

MY SNAIL

At the bottom of my garden
Unaware that he is mine
My snail awaits in his luscious
Green grass.

As he slowly slithers down
My garden path, he leaves
Behind his silver trails
I can follow these.

Suddenly he is attracted to a
Flash of light the glinting
Buckle of my shoe.

As I scoop him up with my
Giant hand and plop him
Into my tub I prod him
And poke him now I feel big
And strong.

As I leave him overnight something
Has gone wrong I put no holes
Into his tub the poor little thing
So what who cares there's plenty more out there.

Louise Whitehouse (10) Manvers Junior School

THE TIGER

He's lying in the grass,
Waiting for the perfect moment,
To pounce upon his prey.
His ears are back,
Straining to hear his,
Prey coming nearer.
His eyes are searching,
Looking for an ideal hunt.

At last the perfect chance,
A young zebra left alone,
Its mother busy eating.
The tiger springs!
The zebra is down,
As the tiger begins to
Eat his kill.

Lucy Clark (10) Manvers Junior School

5, 4, 3, 2, 1 BLAST OFF

10, 9, 8, 7, 6, 5, 4, 3, 2, 1 blast off,
Big red booster rockets,
Like missiles,
Bang! Crash! Boom!
The space shuttle leaves the Earth,
Flaming fire bursts out of the engines,
And up goes the rocket,
The noise of the engines is deafening,
The rocket reaches out for Jupiter,
It is icy cold,
With howling winds,
The planet is bare,
No life is seen,
The rocket stands alone,
The only life is,
The visitors who,
Have landed on the moon.

Jonathan Pratt (11) Manvers Junior School

RHINOCEROS

Why are we in danger?
Why can't we be free,
Just like a human or a bumble bee?

Why do they shoot us?
Why can't we roam peacefully on
our open plains?

Why do they hunt us?
Why do we have to run
Away from the man with a gun?

We should be safe and free.
Allowed to run and roam peacefully
Not hunted to near extinction.

Lee Kirton (10) Manvers Junior School

TIGER IN A ZOO

Backwards and forwards, the tiger softly padded,
In the darkness of his tiny cage.
Then suddenly his dull eyes caught,
A small waver of movement.

Tiredly he pounced into a darkening corner,
Stretching his hardly used muscles.
His movement seemed to trigger a memory,
Of warm stretches of sand, beneath his feet,
Of juicy meals, of newly caught meat.

The memory then faded, he was back in his cage,
Staring at the cold concrete floor.
The bars around him,
Encases him, in his new found home.

Rachael Webster (11) Manvers Junior School

STUCK IN A ZOO

I'm in a cage,
In a zoo,
Looking for something interesting to do.
Everyone looks at me and moves away,
I've been here for months,
Day after day.
I once was happy and roamed free,
Until they came and caught me.
Now I'm stuck in this cage,
A square concrete pen,
All grey, no greenery.
Hardly any fresh food,
It puts me in a bad mood.
I'll never be free,
I'll always be here,
Year after year
Day after day.

Andrew Wilson (11) Manvers Junior School

LION RUG

I'm a lion,
I lived in the forests
now I live in an old house
on the floor, my head is dusty.
I lived in lush green grass,
but now I live on grassless concrete.
It's not fair,
they would not like it,
dead on the forest floor
just a head and skin.

Richard Sentance (11) Manvers Junior School

THE GIANT FISH TANK

Round and round I swim all day
A giant fish tank you could say
I'm a killer of the sea
I'm upset can't you see
Forward flips and through the hoop
It's like I'm in a bowl of soup
I'm fed up of people watching me
Why don't they leave and just let me be?
I hear my family crying out there
But they don't mind they don't care
Oh please let me out
Let me swim about
I remember the time I was with my friend
This is driving me round the bend
But soon some day
I'll get away
With a lot of hope I'll soon be free
Over there like that bird and bee.

Luke Franklin (11) Manvers Junior School

I AM A FILM STAR BUT . . .

I am a film star but . . .
This is my life.
My fin on my back is bent,
I can't swim very far,
I can't swim the ocean free,
I can't catch my own food,
I can't be with others like me!

I'm stuck in a shallow pool.
I'm cooped up all the time,
I get fed for my tricks
A few fish at a time!

No-one realises what it's like,
Not to swim the oceans free.
To be held in captivity,
When I really should be free.

Jo Groom (10) Manvers Junior School

NEVER FORGET

It was the TV that told me that you were splitting up.
I went to my room and sat on my bed
Heartbroken and head spinning,
all I could possibly think about was not seeing
you five hunks sitting on those stools
singing Babe or Everything Changes,
and all the other hits you've written.
I just thought I'd tell you that I'll Never Ever
Forget you Take That
and then it just hit me
My hero my baby was gone
My little Mark Owen was gone he had disappeared
off the face of the earth.
I wish with all my heart that he decides to go
solo or even pair up with Robbie.
I just wish . . .
I'll Never Forget!

Penny Turns (11) Manvers Junior School

HOLIDAY ON THE MOON

If I could choose a place to go
For my holiday in June,
It could be France or it could be Wales
But no, it would be the moon.
There wouldn't be crowds,
Pushing me about and splashing in the pools.
I think there would be a bright pink sea
And mountains covered in jewels.
There would be chocolate flavoured lollipops,
In the shape of trees.
And beautiful flowers made of silk,
Covered in marshmallow bees.
I'd send a postcard from the moon
Saying wish you were here,
I'll see you very soon.
But unhappily I'm staying here
On Earth next year.

Loren Moyes (10) Manvers Junior School

I AM A PARROT

I am a parrot
sitting in a cage
repeating everything,
everything you say.

I miss the wind
against my wings.
I miss the crackling
of the rustling trees.

I sit in here,
day in, day out.
I want to get out
and fly about.

I'm only a parrot
what do you see in me?
All I want
is to be set free!

Andrew Bee (10) Manvers Junior School

THE PLIGHT OF A GENTLE GIANT

Through the peaceful ocean roams,
The gentle giant,
He silent moans.

Lazy waves splash up his hide
Getting stronger
With the tide.

But now we see the mighty chase
The near end
Of a dying race

He dives down deep into the blue
The boat comes near
A harpoon flew.

He flaps around in crimson bath
Gets reeled in
While sailors laugh

Human beings have won
Now all the gentle giants
Have gone.

Charlotte Thomson (10) Manvers Junior School

SKELETON IN MY CUPBOARD

I know there's a skeleton in my cupboard!
I hear him when I'm in bed at night.
I pull the quilt over my head,
And lay trembling, my knees pulled up tight.

I know there's a skeleton in my cupboard!
He rattles his bones late at night.
I try to go to sleep,
And scrunch my eyes up tight.
Hoping to block out the light.
But it's no use,
I know his bony shaped figure is lurking there.

I know there's a skeleton in my cupboard,
He keeps me awake all through the night.
The sun is coming up now,
The bedroom's full of light.
You don't know what it's like,
Having a skeleton keep you awake all night.

There's no longer a skeleton in my cupboard!
I can at last get some rest.
I'm sure my skeleton's afraid of the light,
As I lay down to sleep,
It's finally . . . goodnight!

Jennifer Clark (11) Manvers Junior School

138

THE HUNTER

I saw a shadow of a man,
Hiding behind a tree.
He was holding a gun,
Big and long,
He aimed it straight at me!

He pulled the trigger, aimed at me.
I leapt away, ran up a tree.
The shadow came closer, straight at me.
I hated him like he hated me.

He aimed at me.
I ran further up the tree.
He shot a branch,
and it just missed me!

I leapt out of the tree,
As he started to climb,
I ran away, far, far, far away,
In the hope that distance
would save me.

Lewis Hackett (10) Manvers Junior School

PEREGRINE FALCON

Far up in the air the sun glares
on the sand below.
I think this is the end,
you people drive me round the bend.
You tease me with food,
You make me do things I don't want to do.
You make me look like a toy.
You make money out of me.
But if I were to stop . . . ?

Christian Lewis (11) Manvers Junior School

139

BLACK SILVER BARS

Crunching footsteps, a deadly shot,
Silver guns, an evil plot.
I'm running fast
And then a shot,
The next thing I know
I'm in a zoo,
Just black silver bars
They should be for you.

Craig Hooks (11) Manvers Junior School

THE GLASS BOTTOM BOAT

I stood on the harbour looking out at the sea,
Waiting for the boat that's going to take me,
Away from land, from everything,
I hear an engine hum and sing,
I climb aboard and sit on the side,
Next to the water where secrets lie.
We move off as I look back,
My past life seems very black,
I look down at the waters blue,
Up above a seagull flew.
The green and the blue silently swirl,
The clouds are as white as the mother of pearls.
Soaring back now, the wind in my face,
Soaring back now, at a very fast pace.
I've seen some things I might not see again,
In the boiling hot sunshine,
No sight of rain.
'Land ahoy!' I hear a boy cry,
All the excitement, it starts to die,
Suddenly I'm back standing still in the heat,
Listening to the bustle of trundling feet.

Lindsay Durham (11) Manvers Junior School

ABOVE MY HEAD

Above my head there's a beautiful butterfly,
flying onwards towards my tree.
Oh, oh, oh dear my dad put a net upon the tree,
the butterfly's trapped oh deary me.
The poor orange butterfly,
The poor beautiful orange butterfly.

It breaks free from the net upon the tree,
this beautiful creature is free, free, free.
Upon a rose sits a wonderful butterfly,
that wonderful orange butterfly,
that magnificent orange butterfly,
I'm glad that butterfly is *free.*

Amy Baxter (11) Manvers Junior School

THE PLANET JUPITER

Jupiter the unknown planet,
It doesn't have any life.
A nice mixture of red and white,
To the eyes of us.
It's a mixture of delight.

Jupiter the planet of three moons.
The planet with a hole of mystery.
The mysterious red hole has us
all wondering about it.
Why is it there?
The planet looks a clumsy planet.
The outer skin looks fragile.
As if holes would be easily made.

Andrew Mudie (11) Manvers Junior School

OH LUCY!

My mummy says:
'Oh, Lucy!
I can't leave you alone for five minutes
Without you:
Making a puddle on the toilet floor,
Splashing muddy footprints all over the carpet,
Smashing all the cups and saucers,
Jumping on the bed and breaking all the springs
Knocking over my best plant pot,
Ripping up all of my favourite duvet.

I can't put up with it for any longer,
Do it once more and I'll take you to . . .
Mrs Brown! The child catcher!'

She also says:
'Oh, Lucy!
You've done it again!
Eating most of my newly baked cookies,
Making a mud-pie on the floor,
You've thrown my books all over the living room,
Picked all the leaves off my wonderful plants,

That's it! I'm taking you to Mrs Brown!'

She said nothing else but she:
Whipped me out of the door,
Stepping in the puddle on the toilet floor,
Slipping in the muddy footprints,
Kicking the last remaining saucer,
Knocking over another plant pot,
Tripping over her best duvet,
Crushing all the left over cookies,
Falling on top of the mud-pie,
Stepping on the spines of the books on the floor,
Treading on the stems of the plants.

Maybe she should go to Mrs Brown!

Louise Green (11) Manvers Junior School

THEY'RE TAKING THE MICK

They're taking the mick
I must be thick
I can't catch that silly stick.
You always choose the things I eat
Most of them smell like stinky feet.
Even when I chase a cat
You tell me off while
You pat the cat on the back.
This is cruel
I must be a fool
The cat makes up all the rules
I definitely must be a stupid mutt!

Elizabeth Cowell (11) Manvers Junior School

CAPTIVITY

It is no fun
sitting around in the sun
in this enforced prison
far away from my home
behind bars.
It is not fair
what do they care
with kids staring and glaring.
Why why is it me?
We all should be free.

Matthew Savage (11) Manvers Junior School

GORILLA

It's no fun sitting in the sun
why am I threatened by a gun?
Now I am sitting behind bars listening
to all the cars
people come and stare at me
oh please can someone set me free?

I used to be with all my friends
eating bananas and playing games
now I sit alone all day
nothing to do and nothing to play
is anyone bothered what is happening
to me oh please can I be free?

John Martin (10) Manvers Junior School

BIG BULLY

I'm the big bully,
The biggest of them all
But inside I'm really small
Creeping around the playground all day,
Watch out little fellow,
I'm coming your way,
I'll punch your lights out,
If you stay,
So run along little fellow,
Run along and play,
Hey big bully,
Don't pick on my brother,
Pick on me instead,
But I can't big boy,
And why is that,
Because inside,
I'm really small.

Kirsty Lilliman (10) Newlands Junior School

DOLPHINS

Dolphins swim like a bullet
along they go across the sea.
Smooth silky skin
as soft as anything.
Let's just go for a ride.
More to see than I have ever
seen before.

I wish that I
could be a dolphin.

Michele Froggatt (10) Newlands Junior School

FOREST POEM

F is for the forest around the schools and towns.
O is for the oxygen that makes the world go round.
R is for the raindrops that makes the trees so high.
E is for the energy that trees supply.
S is for the soil around the trees' roots.
T is for the trees that everyone chops down.

P is for the people who live among the town.
O is for the orchids that live beneath the trees.
E is for the evergreen that grows all year round and . . .
M is for the mice that take the berries off plants and trees.

Lee Wood (10) Newlands Junior School

YOU'RE YOU

You're not an 1/8 in a whole
You're not a mountain in a range
You're not a star in the dark night sky
You're not an ear in a field
You're not a page in the Holy Bible
You're not a room in a house
You're not a petal on a flower
You're not a bee in a hive
You're not a hair on a scalp
You're not a cell in a drop of blood
You're not a rock in a pile
You're you.

Shaun Brown (11) Newlands Junior School

MY VALENTINE

I've got a valentine,
but I don't know who it is,
could it be Andy Richardson,
or maybe Marcus Titch.
I think it's John Parker,
or could it be David Johnson?
I hope it's David Johnson.
he's kind of cute.
I told all my friends about it
Oh! This is driving me round the twist.
My very worst nightmare
It was Marcus Titch!

Sarah Barker (11) Newlands Junior School

ONE BEAUTIFUL MORNING

One beautiful morning the flowers started
to grow. The sun was shining on the ground.
I could hear a bluetit singing in the garden.

The amazing poppies and the sunflowers
moved to the wind. The people were
having a picnic on the field.

The trees were blossoming in the garden,
The blossoms were falling on the ground.

Melissa Hopkinson (10) Newlands Junior School

MORNING

In the morning the birds sing me their
morning chorus, while the sun slowly rises
above the hills in the distance. The sunrise is
wonderful all the colours submerge, the sun's
aura glows in the morning sky. Every day I watch
it rise, every day it looks more beautiful. It
brings light and a new beginning to all the
world.

Jemma Lee-Fenyn (11) Newlands Junior School

MY RABBIT

Little rabbit soft and warm,
Round and cuddly,
Just been born,
Eats all the grass on your father's lawn,
And when they shout you wish you weren't born,
Little rabbit made me weep,
When I thought you were lost you'd burrowed so deep,
Leaving behind a fine muddy heap.

Now my rabbit is big and old,
Likes to be free and not to be held,
It likes to be stroked and never to be poked,
And likes to snuggle down in my furry coat,
Sometimes I wish I'd had a cat,
But I'm glad I didn't for I love my rabbit and that's a fact!

Jade Andrews (10) Northfield Junior School

THE TRAMP

He sits in the park all day through
Not having much to do.
He is quite strange people do say
But he's never harmed anyone in any way.
He walks to the litter bin all alone
But there's nothing to eat
Not even a bone.
As he grows older and the days go on
The children in the park
Still play on.
His face is dirty
His clothes are too
Bet you're glad it isn't you?
Where he lives is cold and damp
But then he's just a lonely old *tramp*.

Anna Morrison (10) Northfield Junior School

SPRING

Spring is almost here,
Crocuses start to appear.
No more icy hills,
Just yellow daffodils.
Goodbye to the big freeze,
Hello to lovely green trees.

Babies are taken out in their prams,
Hoping to see the new born lambs.
Chicks are hatching from their shells,
How I love the flowering smells.
Can't wait for sunny days,
With a warm glowing haze.

Lisa Marie Bennett (10) Northfield Junior School

149

SPRING

Spring is the time for animals,
the time for the sun to shine
the sun is strong, it blinds
the weather is fine nobody minds
Me and my mates are playing football and
Rugby but I just hate it when the bugs
bug me.
The flowers are growing like the winds
blowing
In the winter people were sewing
But me and my dad are rowing down the
Stream
Now is the time for ice-creams
Now is the time winter has gone
Don't we all love spring
Well we do anyway

Christopher Maxfield (10) & Michael Smith (11) Northfield Junior School

SPRINGTIME

Flowers bloom,
No more gloom,
Spring is here at last,
Birds sing,
Churchbells ring,
Now winter is in the past,
Now we play,
Sun shines all day,
I hope it's going to last,
Mum and dad are happy,
My sister's gone wappy,
But never mind summer will be here fast.

Laura Henson : Northfield Junior School

BADGERS

Badgers are fierce not cuddly toys
Badgers are creeping not making a noise
Badgers have stripes and black and white faces
Badgers come out at night
There's one thing that badgers do
Is come looking for you.

Nichola Makings (8) Northfield Junior School

THE RAINBOW

Red and yellow, pink and green,
In a rainbow every colour can be seen.
Orange, purple and blue,
With every colour there's something to do.
Bright sparkles fill the sky
And you can see all of the rainbow
in my eye.

Debbie Bancroft (9) Northfield Junior School

BADGERS

Badgers are cuddly so furry and soft
My mate stripy is super and soft
He is quite friendly people do say
I wish he would come and play
He's cute he's big he's my kind of mate
In fact I think my badger's great.

Stephanie Morrison (8) Northfield Junior School

THE SEA

The sea is very calm today
It's because the sun's warm today
If I look carefully I might see
A fish, swim swim swimming away.

The sea is very rough today
It's nothing like yesterday
No ships can sail far away
The sea is much too rough today.

The sea is quite calm today
Thank goodness it's not like yesterday
So I can swim and swim today
Swim from mum far far away.

Anna Desforges (10) Northfield Junior School

GEORGE THE DRAGON

George the dragon had golden scales,
Eyes as big as silver pails,
Smoke filling all the sky,
Making all the children cry.

George the dragon was very charming,
But when he was angry he was most alarming,
Breathing fire everywhere,
George he didn't seem to care.

George the dragon was very alarmed,
When people said they might be harmed,
George said he was very sorry,
He didn't mean to cause them worry.

Natalie Fadden (11) Northfield Junior School

152

SPRING!

Springtime
The ground becomes
awake
Primroses and
daffodils bloom
after the winter's break,
Rabbits hopping along
the ground.
I wonder if there are
any Easter eggs to be found.
Nests being built by a
bird in a tree.
Green shoots
appearing wherever the
eye can see.

Jonathan Timmons (10) Northfield Junior School

MY BABY SISTER

I've got a new baby sister
She is very very nice
She has her milk
And burps a lot and hardly ever cries.

She's got some pretty dresses
She looks very very sweet
And loves to go in her new pram
A walk down the street

She has a favourite teddy that plays
Music as she sleeps
Her name is Chloe June
And she's my sister for keeps.

Leah Gibson (8) Northfield Junior School

153

ANIMALS AT RISK

Animals in danger are going to be extinct,
If we never learn to think.
Tigers, elephants and leopards too,
If we keep killing them what shall we do?
We are so stupid, we kill them every minute
of the day,
We should not get our own way,
Lions, monkeys, cheetahs too
Surely this is not the right thing to do.
All the animals in the world,
Should be free.
If we never learn to think,
We will never learn to link together,
forever.

Laura Bostock (11) Northfield Junior School

THE VIKING SHIP

A ship in the sea,
A storm is to be,
The storm is starting,
The sailors go darting,
The wind is screaming,
The lightning's gleaming,
The oars are smashed,
And so is the mast,
From the dreadful storm,
That has just been born,
It starts to get light,
Every soul with frost bite,
Then at last the storm is over.

Samantha Land (10) Northfield Junior School

154

THE MONSTER BEHIND THE LOO

The monster behind the loo
Isn't there
Till you sit on the ring of the seat
And just when you're in
The middle of things,
A spider scuttles down the wall
A daddy long legs pays a call
A moth flies off the toilet roll
And the monster
Scuffles
Its
Feet!

Andrew Smith : Northfield Junior School

WIND

On a very scary, scary night,
I approach the house,
Windows rattling,
Bin bags falling,
I'm as quiet as a mouse,
I slip through the door,
Snatching things to join me.
Soon I'm like a raving lion
I jump to the roof,
I can't get it off!
So I drive away from this disgrace.
I push, I pull
Everywhere.
You won't stop me . . .
Beware!

Elliot Zaccaria (9) North Wheatley Primary School

BUTTERFLY

Bright colours
Flying in the air.
Delicate,
Light,
Breakable.
Hovering over the flowers,
Attractive to the eye.
Fly away
Then . . . like . . .
a . . . leaf . . . falling . . .
from . . . a . . . tree . . .
Crash!
Into the spider's web
That's the end of me.

Oliver Whitehurst (8) North Wheatley Primary School

THE WIND

All is calm,
Then all of a sudden,
The wind starts to blow . . .
The grass is flapping from side to side.
Trees start creaking
Milk bottles crash
People hurrying home
Water rippling.
Then off he goes quietly to see where else
he can blow.

Laura Ann Bacon (8) North Wheatley Primary School

DRAGON BEAT

Dragon roar, roar, roar,
Echoing down the hill.
See the dragon soar, soar, soar,
Stopping and lying still.

Come and see his dragon feet,
Dancing on the ground.
Tapping to the beat,
Twirling round and round.

Boiling, bubbling, orange flames,
Floating everywhere.
Dragon likes playing games,
Smoke is in the air.

Cooking people's toast,
Sausages as well.
Frying the Sunday roast,
What a lovely smell.

Laura Ogley (9) North Wheatley Primary School

MY BARMY BODY

On my leg is a washing peg.
On my chin is a rubbish bin.
On my nose are ten smelly toes.
On my eyes are ten hundred pies.
On my hair is a cuddly bear.
On my chest is a pongy mess.
On my feet is some meat.
On my knee is a bee.
On my ear is a pint of beer.

Frances Stanton (7) Porchester Junior School

MY NUMBER POEM

One orange otter
Two toys on a television
Three trains on a track
Four flat flies
Five fine fingers
Six sticky stickers
Seven slimy slugs
Eight Easter eggs
Nine nasty nets
Ten terrible tunnels.

Natalie Wheelhouse (8) Porchester Junior School

FOOTBALL POEM

Three o'clock Saturday afternoon
The match was about to start
The supporters steamed up Wembley Way
Which team would win the cup today?

Forest in red, Luton in white
Forest scored the first goal alright!
Ducking and diving, weaving and wangling
Who will be the next to score?

The crowd go wild
Forest have won
They scored nine
While Luton had none!

Joseph Poyzer (10) Porchester Junior School

THINGS COULD BE WORSE

A tree could fall on my head.
A dog could eat King Kong.
A cat could eat two thousand dogs.
But it gets even worse.
A poltergeist could take the world.
My cat could eat a dictionary and start
talking clever.
But now comes the gruesome bit.
I could be sick out of my ear, mouth and
nose.

James Dames (8) Porchester Junior School

MY SEA POEM

The sea is like a wild, raging pony.
But under the sea,
Is a different place to be,
The trembling, tired, lost seahorse child seeks
a scrap of food.
The tiny crabs scuttle around and gently
dance on the rocks till sundown.
The irresistible golden sand,
Fades and the waves calm down,
But in the morning it all starts up again,
The crashing, bashing, smashing waves, shriek
And scream at the sand and rocks.
Dragons roar at the sun in the sky,
Telling her 'You're too bright!'
The sunset is a paint palette of golden
Red and brown,
Now the sea is calm again, like a soft
And silky gown.

Kelly Ruston (11) Porchester Junior School

WHAT IS COLOUR

What is red?
Red is an angry face.
Red is a nasty evil devil.

What is green?
Green is a shining forest.
Green is leaves rustling on the trees.

What is pink?
Pink is a happy rose.
Pink is a royal ruby laying
in the sun.

What is blue?
Blue is a boring sad old colour.
Blue is a shining happy sky.

What is yellow?
Yellow is a big happy lemon.
Yellow is a hot sun that shines
down on me.

Amanda Dracott (8) Porchester Junior School

SLOWLY

Slowly the sun rises over the hill,
Slowly the stream drips water on a fish
Slowly the paint brush paints a beautiful picture
Slowly the light switches on and off
Slowly I dive into the pool
Slowly my footsteps follow me
Slow as a snail but slowest of all
The garden growing near the old brass door.

Jemma Clewley (8) Porchester Junior School

THE CREEPY NIGHTMARE

The stars blinked like a lovely lady
And the sky was pretty and bright.
The shadows sneezed like an old man
But no-one heard him.

The bird sang like a beautiful girl
And every one loved it.
The door quivered like a cold girl
But no-one could see it.

The trees rustled like a cold child
But everyone was cold.
The trees whipped me like an old head master
And it hurt me.

Lucy Hingley (8) Porchester Junior School

KELLY PIKE'S RAP

Hi everybody. Look at me, I'm Kelly Pike the bumble bee!
A hip hop a hip hop
Come on everybody do the bumble bee rap!

Buzz around your kitchen,
Buzz around your floor,
Buzz around everybody,
Make your grandpa snore.

A hip hop a hip hop rap
Come on everybody, do
The bumble bee rap, yeah!

Kelly Pike (9) Porchester Junior School

MY BARMY BODY

On my hair
Is a big brown bear.

On my arm
Is a stinky farm.

On my nail
Is a wiggly snail.

On my lip
Is a orange pip.

On my shoulder
Is a pint of lager.

On my chest
Is a dirty nest.

Laura McMasters (7) Porchester Junior School

THE ROARING SEA

The bottle green waves smash in my face,
And wash me away without a trace,
I find myself being carried away,
By these waves of different array,
Some are blue,
Some are green,
Some are very seldom seen
But one did roar,
One did thrash,
It would wreck a yacht with one summoned smash!
It never gives mercy,
It never feels pain,
Its thrashes feel like a hand after the cane!

Harley Kemp (10) Porchester Junior School

MY BARMY BODY

On my knee
Is a chimpanzee
On my tum
Is a big bass drum

On my feet
Is a giant piece of meat
On my arm
There's a massive farm

On my nose
There are some frozen toes
On my toes
There's a dead rose

On my hair
There's a giant bear.

Thomas Hackett (8) Porchester Junior School

IN THE LAND OF SNOBLEY MOO

In the land of Snobley Moo
You will see a big round loo

In the land of Snobley Moo
you will see a plop of goo

In the land of Snobley Moo
Everyone wears slimy shoes

In the land of Snobley Moo
The people are covered in glue

In the land of Snobley Moo
Everybody shouts boo!

Adam Grundy (8) Porchester Junior School

THE 4 RAPPERS. THE NAUGHTY SCHOOL RAP

When I was one I burnt down the school,
When I was two I got detention,
When I was three I got expelled,
When I was four I got my pension.

Hip, hop, hip, hop, hap, I'm giving you the four rappers' rap.

When I was five I did a dive,
When I was six I sang out live,
When I was seven I went to Heaven,
When I was eight I ate a plate,
When I was nine the world was mine,
When I was ten I killed a hen.

Hip, hop, hip, hop, hap I'm giving you the four rappers' rap.

James Morgan, Daniel Blake, Jason Oliver (9), Simon Leonard (8)
Porchester Junior School

SAD, SLAVE POEM

S   low that's what I'm not,
    Because my master orders me to get cleaning on the dot!

L   eave, that's what I'd like to do,
    Before my master shouts, 'Slave, where are you?'

A   s frightened as a mouse caught in a trap,
    That's what I'm like, but when I'm brave, I'm as blave as a pike!

V   ast, that's what I'd wish to be,
    To squish my master like a flea.

E   nergy is what I need,
    To complete the tasks that I receive.

Chelsea Harris (10) Porchester Junior School

THE ANIMAL RAP

Get it written
If you don't you will get bitten
Every body listen to me
If you don't you will come to me

Hip hop hip hop hap

I'm giving you all the animal rap
When I was one I had a frog
When I was two I had a dog
When I was three I had a bee
When I was four I had a parrot
When I was five I had a fish
When I was six I had a bear
When I was seven I had a snail
When I was eight I had a snake
When I was nine they made me king of the cats
I'm giving you all the animal rap.

Keisha Makanjuola (9) Porchester Junior School

THE WIND THAT SCREAMED

The wind screamed like a crying baby.
But the shadows danced like a singing ballet-dancer.
The moonlight shone like a twinkle star.
And the clouds moved like a shaking carpet
The sea cried like a crying wolf
But the forest roared like a bad bear.
And the bird died like a crying boy
The desert crashed like a howling lion
But the fish sank like a sad dog.

Kelly Powell (9) Porchester Junior School

165

THE YEARS' RAP

A hip, hop, hip, hop, hap I'm giving you all the Scott and Kyle rap.
When I was 1 I made a song,
When I was 2 it all went wrong!
When I was 3 I got no attention.
When I was 4 (I don't want to mention),
that I had to start school.

A hip, hop, hip, hop, hap I'm giving you all the Scott and Kyle rap.
When I was 5 I beat up all the kids,
When I was 6 I played the drums on dustbin lids.
When I was 7 I robbed a bank with my brother.
When I was 8 I had my fate.

A hip, hop, hip, hop, hap, I'm giving you all the Scott and Kyle rap.
When I was 9 I won the pools.
When I was 10 they made me king of the fools.
A hip, hop, hip, hop, hap, and now you've listened to the Scott and Kyle rap.

Kyle Denoon (9) & Scott Lumley (8) Porchester Junior School

A SCARY NIGHT

The desert stood still like a statue.
But the sea moaned like someone crying for help.
The shadows crept like a spooky ghost.
But the storm crashed like a pair of cymbals
The waves swayed like the trees.

The stream froze like an ice-cube.
But the forest danced like a ballerina.
The wind whistled like a teacher blowing her whistle.
But the darkness whispered like a scared child.
The moonlight sang like a robin.

Lindsey Kate Burke (9) Porchester Junior School

THE WIND SMASHES

The wind whistled like a bird.
But the shadows quivered like a cat.
The forest screamed like a wolf.
And the sea moaned like a baby.
The darkness crept like a hedgehog.
But the clouds froze like a statue.
The desert crashed like thunder.
And the waves sank like sand.
The stream smiled like the sun.
But the elephants crashed like lightening.
The moonlight froze like a bird.
And the birds flew like a silent wind.
The crocodiles smash like trees.
But the wind grew like a giraffe.

Christopher Pearson (8) Porchester Junior School

ON MY BARMY BODY

On my ear
Is a big pint of beer
On my chin
Is a lovely thin pin

On my arm
Is a house alarm
On my feet
Is a smelly old sheet

On my hair
Is a little green pear
On my chest
Is a wooden vest.

Mathew Overton (8) Porchester Junior School

167

SADNESS IS . . .

Sadness is as cruel as a teacher.
Sadness is as angry as a lion
Sadness is as miserable as the roaring sea.
Sadness is as unhappy like a boy not allowed to play out.
Sadness is upset as the burning sun.

Happiness is as happy as a swimming fish
Happiness is as helpful as a paper boy
Happiness is funny like a laughing clown

Loneliness is as sad as the moon
Loneliness is horrible like a rainy day
Loneliness is as cruel as a computer

Cruelness is as horrible as a robber.
Cruelness is as haunted as a witch.
Cruelness is as sad as an angry sun.

Dwane Oakey (9) Porchester Junior School

SADNESS IS . . .

Sadness is as lonely as the moon in the night sky
Sadness is as angry as a roaring lion in a
                          lonely cage with all the people looking.
The sun is as destructive as a nuclear bomb ready to go off
Bang
Sadness is as cruel as a red snake ready to pounce on your leg.
Fear is as frightening as an animal ready
To go to the butcher's
To be killed.

Sean Rawson (9) Porchester Junior School

SADNESS IS . . .

Sadness is like the angry waves going in and out.
Sadness is like the lonely trees ruffing.
Sadness is like the glittering moon floating up in the sky.
Sadness is like the burning sun hanging in the sky.
Sadness is like the beautiful stars shining in the night.

Stephen Bullick (8) Porchester Junior School

SADNESS IS SO TERRIBLE

Sadness is as lonely as a
Candle flame flickering in the
Darkest nights.
Sadness is as cruel as a bomb falling
On innocent children.
Sadness is as upset as a dying
Flower which has been blossoming until
The cruel winter frosts.
Sadness is as terrible as a young
Life that has been taken by cruel wars.

Sadness is as angry as the
Raging waves crashing against the
Rocks and sand.
Sadness is as grumpy as
The thumping hailstones banging
On children's heads.
Sadness is as miserable as
The loneliness of a young child lost
In a place full of people.
Sadness is as destructive
As a fire creeping in houses to
Kill innocent people.

Elizabeth Mary Abbott (9) Porchester Junior School

169

SLAVES

A slave is for a person to keep,
Bound with chains around his feet,
To serve a master for every day,
For just a very little pay,
Slaves were really not meant to be,
Everyone in life should be free.

Damian Charles Gray (10) Porchester Junior School

MY SCARY POEM

The sea moaned at the beach,
As the sun sank into the clouds,
Darkness grew nearer
As the light died in pain,
And I felt scared.

The cave beckoned me towards,
The shadowy figure inside it,
As the wind howled behind me,
And I felt scared.

The trees whispered in the darkness
Corrupting the silence in the forest,
Eyes in the darkness
Peering through the shadows in silence,
And I felt scared.

The sun cried
As it sunk into the clouds
And I felt scared.

Lucy Woodman (10) Porchester Junior School

MY COLOUR POEM

What is blue?
Blue is when I miss my mum.
Blue is when I miss my dad.
Blue is the colour of the sea,
Swimming pool and the sky.
Blue is also a colour.

What is white?
White is a colour of snow.
White is when someone isn't very well.
White is the colour of towels we use.
White is the colour of the rubbers we use too.
And white is also a colour.

What is yellow?
Yellow is the colour of the inside of the eggs we eat.
Yellow is the colour of the rising sun.
Yellow is the colour of the welcoming fire.
Yellow is also a colour.

What is red?
Red is when I am mad.
Red is when I blush.
Red is when I am upset.
Red is also a colour.

Michelle Rossitter (10) Porchester Junior School

SLAVE POEM

A slave is as lonely as an empty playground.
A slave is as sad as a homeless kitten lost on a dark stormy night.
A slave is as poor as a tramp with no home.
A slave is as trapped as a robber in jail.
A slave is as frightened as a tiny boy lost in the wood.
A slave is as unhappy as a small child with no family.
A slave is as terrified as a lovely kitten stuck in a tree.

Sean Hendry (10) Porchester Junior School

AUTUMN DAYS

Leaves in the air
Leaves everywhere
Leaves blowing around
On the ground
Rainy misty
Terrible weather
Fires on,
Soups boiling
Slippers on
I'm getting
Warmer.
Football matches
On the park
Better get
Finished
Before it's
Dark.

Ben Brodsky (10) Porchester Junior School

DIZZY RAP

Hip hop, hip, hop hap
I'm giving you all
The dizzy work rap

When I was one, I had no tongue
When I was two, I had a poo
When I was three, I had a bee
When I was four, I was so poor
Hip, hop, hip, hop, hap,
When I was five, I had a hive
When I was six, I ate a Twix
When I was seven, I went to heaven
When I was eight, I ate a plate,
When I was nine, I had a fine
When I was ten, I ate a pen.

Craig Norman (8) Porchester Junior School

AUTUMN DAYS

The rain is falling
on the windowpane,
the big log fire is flickering
up and down.
The sparrows are
twittering,
the morning light.
Suddenly a storm is
beginning to blow
the oak tree's leaves.

Adam Denoon (11) Porchester Junior School

AUTUMN POEM

The windy breeze of
Autumn arrival.
The crispy leaves and
Misty streets.
The conkers falling,
October arrives.
The frosty trees the
Snow in sight.
The birds are
Migrating the
Fruit is ripe for picking
And eating to make
Pies that are nice.
The leaves are falling
Off the trees,
Changing colours, crumbling
At my feet.
The cold air that passes
By you.
The squirrels running
Around gathering nuts
For winter.

Kerrie O'Neill (11) Porchester Junior School

THE RIVER

The river freezes in winter and sparkles in summer.
It flows swiftly downstream
Down waterfalls and over rocks
Down the winding bends like nothing stops it and splashes into the sea at last.

Hollie Morris (11) Porchester Junior School

VICKY'S FAB POEM

The sea roared like an angry lion.
But a lion wasn't there.
The bird sang like a person
And every bird joined in
The shadow crept up on me
And it made me fall over.
The sun was begging me to come out
But I did not go out
The jungle crept up on me when I was walking
But I did not fall over
The sun burnt me when I was playing
But no-one knew I was burnt by the sun.

Victoria Boultby (8) Porchester Junior School

MY BARMY BODY

On my ear
Is a pint of beer
On my nose
Is a big dead rose

On my arm
Is a smelly farm
On my bum
Is a pint of rum.

On my feet
Is a slice of meat
On my hips
Is a plate of chips.

Aaron Tyler (8) Porchester Junior School

MY BARMY BODY

On my knee is a bumble bee
On my eye is a giant butterfly.

On my belly is some raspberry jelly.
On my nose are some ugly crows.

On my shoulder is a boulder
On my legs are some eggs
On my toes is a nose.

John Neale (8) Porchester Junior School

A STORMY POEM OF AUTUMN

The leaves are blowing around looking for
Somewhere to land
It starts to snow
Suddenly a strong storm
Starts to blow rubbish about
Birds try to fly away
But the storm is too strong
The birds land
People lock their doors and windows
The storm gets madder and madder
Until thunder and lightning hit the house.
Trees are blowing lots and lots of leaves
Away onto the streets
Water is rushing away
Down into the drains
It starts to hail down with hailstones
Hitting the windows with a smash
The next day the storm calms down.
A rainbow appears.

Kevin Haw (10) Porchester Junior School

MY BARMY BODY

On my head is a
Big fat shed
On my knee is a grand flea

On my chin
Is a wooden bin
On my arm
Is a stinky farm

On my nose is
A frozen rose
On my hair
Is a juicy bear.

Alex Lindley (8) Porchester Junior School

JUNGLE POEM

In the jungle snakes rattle
Sliding through the grass
In the jungle lions roar
Scaring people off
In the jungle hunters sing
With their guns and swords
But then a crash of thunder
Comes
The hunters go home to their wives
The snakes all hide in the grass
And the lions run away.

Natasha Dames (10) Porchester Junior School

THE RIVER

The river threads its way through the hills
In waterfalls and in rock pools
It goes through the valleys sparkling bright.
It starts to rain
All is quiet
Except for the pitter patter of the rain.
It stops raining
All is calm
The river starts to flow fast
With fish jumping up and down
Children and animals come out to
Play.

Emma Roberts (11) Porchester Junior School

RIVERS

Rivers swaying from side to side,
Glistening creatures swimming by.
People walking on the muddy banks
Beavers making their dams today.
People trying to play.
The rivers travelling through valleys.
All the water travelling through.

Marc Stone (10) Porchester Junior School

THE RIVER

In the river live fish.
That like to play about.
They play with the frogs
And the frogs play on the lily pads
Ducks swim around and flap
Their wings about and splash
In the water to wash themselves.
Then the beavers come along
They start to play with other beavers
They all play together in the river.

Rebecca Doubleday (9) Porchester Junior School

RIVER POEM

Rivers glow in the bright night sky
Owls come out and give a cry
Look at the crystal clear water sparkling away
Come on owls come and catch your prey

Animals come and drink
Children throw stones and they sink
People can bathe
Rivers sometimes make a cave.

Anthony Bullick (10) Porchester Junior School

THE RIVER POEM

The river is long the river
Is wide. The people come with
Boats to have a ride. The fish
Get caught by fisherman. The river
Flows through valleys and streams.
The river stops at the sea. The river
Can flow fast or slow.
Wherever it goes the river will know.

Dean Wheatley (10) Porchester Junior School

LAKES

If the sun is shining or the
Rain is pouring, the river doesn't
Care it just keeps on flowing.
To the wide big sea. Its
Friend is there to greet it.
They keep on flowing side by side
They flow fast because all they
Started with is a stream. So
Just keep the rivers clean and
They will do the rest.

Jacqueline Smith (11) Porchester Junior School

PEBBLES

White with black spots like a Dalmatian,
Slight grey blotches behind
Smooth as clear glass,
Dots of orange here and there.

One stone with lots inside,
Smooth as a polished table top.
Stones of all sizes and shapes
Some as white as snow,
A few grey as thunder clouds.

Smooth with a crack in
Dark, sandy gold in colour,
Reddy brown from bottom to top,
Pebbles lying on the beach, stranded.

Sally Cullis (10) Rise Park Junior School

DUNKIRK BEACH - 1940

I felt afraid and proud,
The sun brushing on my face,
The sea was light,
Sea birds
In the clear blue sky.
The smoke getting grey and black,
It makes me happy and sad,
Fishes swimming around,
The men look tired and sad,
All holding their guns.

Aimee Mitchell (11) Rise Park Junior School

MY DAD'S ADDICTED TO TEA

I walked into the living room,
Unaware of what would happen,
When -
'Rachael, make me a cup of tea!'
I ran up the stairs,
As fast as I could,
When -
'Rachael, make me a cup of tea!'
I was sitting in the living room,
Trying to relax,
When -
'Rachael, make me a cup of tea!'
I was sitting in my room,
Watching TV,
When -
'Rachael, make me a cup of tea!'
I was sitting in the kitchen,
Doing my homework,
When -
'Dad, make *me* a cup of tea!'

Rachael Beeson (10) Rise Park Junior School

THE GREEN VIOLINIST

Brown and white are his clothes,
Like times from long ago,
Green face like algae so dark,
And blue hair is like deep sea,
The violin seems to be alive,
Old fashioned houses there,
Jumpers like rows of roses,
The scent is in the air.

Tara Ricketts (11) Rise Park Junior School

182

ICE HOCKEY

The head coach calls my name,
Skate, skate, skate.
On I jump, over the boards,
Skate, skate, skate.
The black puck comes to me,
Skate, skate, skate.
I take it past the opposing players,
Skate, skate, skate.
I'm clean through on the goalie,
Skate, skate, skate.
I try to take it round him,
Skate, skate, skate.
I rip a hole in the net,
Goal! Goal! Goal!

Andrew Makings (11) Rise Park Junior School

HEALTHY EXERCISE

Sky blue,
Open field,
Trees green,
Hills steep,
Fat man,
Rosy cheeks,
Riding a bike,
Taking dog,
For a walk,
Dog has patch,
Black as ink,
Comfy clothes,
Jolly day,
Like a dream.

Adil Lone (11) Rise Park Junior School

183

DUNKIRK - 1940

Boat fast,
Wind blowing in face,
Spraying salt water in mouth, eyes,
The wind refreshing.
Scared, anxious,
Got to hurry.
Black smoke like fire.
Black smudge on beach
It was individual men,
Realised men being shipped home.
More men from sand dunes,
Hurt, unstable.
Boats going back and forth
Like parcels being packed,
Getting men.
Decided to join them.
Pulled first hurt, tired man in boat.
His hand felt cold as terror.

Charlotte Foster (10) Rise Park Junior School

I WISH I WAS A BIRD

I wish I could fly like a bird in the sky
Every moment I feel the clouds going over my mind
When the wind goes by I feel that it's time for bed time.
I hear an owl hoot, hooting every night.
One night a bird came down.
I fell in love
A nest in the tree. Four baby birds cried.

Claire Millington (9) Rise Park Junior School

PEBBLES AND SHELLS

Black stone, streaks as white as a cloud,
Smooth as ice,
Gray lines overlapping white,
Murky black in the background,
Dark as night.

Scallop shell,
Orange as bright as sunset,
Hinges of black and pinky white,
Purple spreads behind the shell.

Pebble in my hand, black as ebony,
Lines in greyish white, smooth as a book cover,
Turn to a white background,
Black lines,
With golden yellow patches around.

Scott Smith (11) Rise Park Junior School

MIRK WOOD

Mirk wood is dangerous and dark. A
mysterious place weird, creepy with massive
spiders' webs, really big bats, moths like
birds the way they glide.

The airless forest. The great eyes which are
red, yellow, green - huge eyes. It is quiet;
you can hear a pin drop. Spooky squirrels'
shadows in the darkness.

Steven Pinegar (9) Rise Park Junior School

MY VIOLIN

I do not know how to play a violin,
Squeak, squeak every time I play,
The cat hides under my bed,
Dad goes barmy, mum goes nuts.

I am sad to say I cannot play,
Squeak, squeak every time I play,
But I try, which is more than the other girls
In my class do.

Mum said, there is a band playing,
I said, I wanted to play my violin,
Squeak, squeak every time I play.
Mum said, you had better practise.

One day came, I took my violin along.
No squeak, squeak,
I could play.
Three cheers for Claire the next day.

Claire Fiona Stimpson (8) Rise Park Junior School

WORMS

Worms worms in the ground
If you look they can't be found.
They only come out in the rain,
If you chop them they're in pain,
But the front comes back alive again.
Off they go home once more,
Even though they're rather sore.

Richard Crofts (11) Rise Park Junior School

186

A BOY

A boy played out merry and bright,
Until he knew there would be lunch tonight,
For the hungry hungry dog next door
With dribbling jaws and slobber,
It gave him such a bore.
Now this boy was very spoilt,
Not polite, but rude,
Seeing he couldn't have a dog
Brought him in a mood
The dog ran down the gloomy streets
And ate him in one go,
That shows you what rudeness can do
To children just like you!

Kayleigh Garratt (10) Rise Park Junior School

MIRKWOOD

Eyes-bulbous, big eyes
flip flap wings from bats and moths
Pitch black scuffling feet
Airless black, deadly river
Black squirrels leap from tree to tree
Pitch black everywhere
Only a glimpse of light here and there
Shadows, a dark green
Great big cobwebs
Very dim
Very quiet
Incredible eerie noises
Frightening sounds.

Rachael Stephenson (9) Rise Park Junior School

GHOST OF THE HALL

Ghost of the hall, it actually scared us
When we were playing basketball.
Then we went into service,
And it made everyone nervous.
Then we went into class and it followed us.
We went out to games and it
Shouted 'James!'
And called him names.

Craig Stewart (10) Rise Park Junior School

DINNER TIME

Going to dinner gives me the creeps.
Going to dinner is the worst of all.
It is even worse when you have to eat it all.
School custard is the worst of all.

Daniel Whittingham (10) Rise Park Junior School

THE ZOO

There are lots of animals at the zoo,
There's a bear that talks and goes boo,
Also there's a giraffe that's 8 feet tall,
And when I stand next to it I look so small,
And there's a monkey that's always around,
And hangs from a tree then climbs back down.
When it's time to go home I'm not
glad, so I pour coffee all down my dad!

Laura Johnson (9) Rise Park Junior School

DRIFTING

I wander through the dense wood lost
Scream from far away
Silences all around, eerie feeling in the sky.
I wander on, it leads me on.
Turned round the corner, a hundred of them gathered,
Oh what a fright.
They were drifting like the clouds in the sky,
Far far away.

Jennifer Houghton (10) Rise Park Junior School

TOM

My best friend, his name is Tom.
He likes to eat a popadom.
His girlfriend's name it is Louise.
He can beat Matthew up with ease.
He sits next to Richard.
But Richard always hits him.
Tom likes the X-files.
He can run for miles.
Tom is quite small.
He is not tall at all.
Tom has a bust-up thumb.
And when he did it, it was numb.
Tom has a foster brother.
He was adopted by his mother.
Tom is really a jolly good mate.
He's asked Louise out on a date.

Adrian Swann (11) Rise Park Junior School

THE SPIDER

There's a spider in our house.
It lurks in every corner
Where we go we always find the spider.
It goes in dark and light places.
When we see the spider it gets us frightened.
We see the spider everywhere
Sometimes making a web
We know the spider's there.

Mark Clayton (10) Rise Park Junior School

DUNKIRK AHEAD

I have to go! But why?
What about mum and dad?

The wind blows in my face.
The water hits my back.
But I don't care,
I have got to go!

The salty spray in my eyes.
But I don't care,
I have got to go!

The smoke puffing, the guns rumbling.
But I don't care,
I have got to go!

The sand crunches,
As the boat lands on the beach.
But I don't care,
I have got to go.

Gemma Harrison (10) Rise Park Junior School

THE THING

It slithers up your bedroom wall,
It crashes through the garage door,
It eats up people big and small,
It feeds on brains,
And he'll like yours!
It can open bedroom doors,
Eat whole people,
And climb up walls,
Splat!
The thing.

Anthony Archer (11) Rise Park Junior School

GOODBYE KISS

I'm heading for the door
Am I going to make it?
I open the door.
There stands my friend.
My mum's behind me.
Her lips are getting ready.
I try to get out the door.
She's gripping my arm.
It's all happening so fast.
The lips are jumping out of her head,
And onto my face.
The brightest red lipstick.
The mark on my face.
It's so embarrassing in front of my friend.
When we get out of the door.
My friend starts laughing at me.
In the outside I'm smiling
On the inside I just want to scream!

Tara Broady (11) Rise Park Junior School

191

PLAY TIME

When it is time for us to play.
All the teachers shout, 'Hooray!'
Into the staff room they flee,
To eat biscuits and drink tea,
They go to the fridge to keep them cold,
They pick their noses (I've been told)
They do handstands against the wall,
Then they play catch with a ball,
Why they do that,
No-one knows.
They play twister and wear wigs,
They watch play-school and eat like pigs,
They bring their beds and go to sleep,
Then they snore and do not peep,
They have discos and hang from lights,
When children come in, it gives them frights,
Why they do that
No-one knows,
What they do in the staff room,
It just shows!

Carly Stephenson (11) Rise Park Junior School

IN THE MORNING

As I wake up in the morning I hear the sounds of nature,
The birds singing sweetly in the apple tree,
The delicate drops of dew on the green grass swaying in the wind,
Every now and then, a squirrel comes to visit the trees in my garden,
Borrowing a little food for its family.
The cool breeze on a warm morning in spring wakes the sleeping flowers,
All this happiness in my garden in the morning.

Priya Saggar (11) Rise Park Junior School

192

1940 - TO DUNKIRK

Enjoyable feeling,
The wind blowing in my face,
The open landscape
At the horizon.
Sweaty heat,
Cooling wind,
Boats everywhere.
It's as if there's an earthquake,
But no movement.
Oil in beach
No wait -
It's men!
Guns in air
Up on beach.
Crunch, as we hit shore.

Tony Curtis (10) Rise Park Junior School

TEACHER

Teacher! Teacher!
Oh what a horrible teacher!
She tells us off all the time
She makes us work very hard.
While she just sits at her desk
And tells us what to do.
She doesn't help us!
When the boys were being daft
Everybody laughed.

Claire Dale (10) Rise Park Junior School

FROM A RAILWAY CARRIAGE

As I set off in a train, faster I go,
Whizzing past trees, streets.
Sheep here, sheep there,
Train is going everywhere.
I look at cattle, I look at sheep,
People standing by the station,
Waiting for the train to come by.
I hear children passing by.
Shouting and screaming
As the train goes by.
Hills passing by,
Clouds look like they're following the train.
I'm glad I went on the train.
You have a good time on the train.

Heather Cree (9) Rise Park Junior School

FROM A RAILWAY CARRIAGE

How fast I go out of the station is a mystery
With all the people waving at me.
When we were out of the station
A long way away, it was mostly quiet
Just someone and me,
And the world whizzes by
At one hundred miles an hour.

Matthew Wales (10) Rise Park Junior School

FROM A RAILWAY CARRIAGE

Whizzing along the meadows
Faster and faster I go
Up the hills, down the hills,
Through the towns and villages.
Faster than cars and buses I go,
Each station I pass I get one glimpse
And then it's gone.
As I watch the birds
I think, why can't I fly?

As I get out of the train at the station
Dizzy and sick,
I get into the car then
It all starts again.

Jamie Heimour (10) Rise Park Junior School

MIRKWOOD

It is spooky, creepy and dark,
It is pitch black, you only see
The eyes of bears, spiders and bats.
Dangerous darkness everywhere,
It is airless and eerie,
Dark, dense cobwebs
Massive insects bigger than you.
It is stuffy and scary.

Darren Watson (9) Rise Park Junior School

195

PEBBLES UPON THE BEACH

Pebbles on a sandy beach.
As smooth as silk.
Like a morning sunrise,
As beautiful as the swaying sea.
A few cracks upon it,
Like a broken shell.
It shines in the light,
It glistens in the sunlight.

Just like an egg, ovally round,
Or like a diamond, smooth and shiny.
Like waves roaring back and forth,
Just like a dreary night,
Dark, quiet, with no light in sight.
Shiny as can be.

Like millions of blue pen marks,
On a creamy complex.
Like a Dalmatian's coat.
Smooth, shiny, almost perfect.
Close to superb.

Just like a sand of its own,
Almost with pebbles of its own,
Browns, yellows, reds, whites,
Even speckles of black.

As I collected these stones
I walked on home.

Lindsey Palmer (10) Rise Park Junior School

CRAB'S LEG

The smell, the smell
Of the left-over figure of the crab's leg.
It is rough and uneven.
I can imagine the whole crab,
Although it's only a leg.
Imagine it moving
As a machined object
Cutting through water at sea.

David Cripwell (10) Rise Park Junior School

MY MUM AND DAD ON HOLIDAY

Mum and dad go to Cyprus
I am very sad
I have dreams and nightmares
I wish I was there
They came safely back to England
I am very glad.

Lee Bennett (9) Rise Park Junior School

MIRKWOOD

Dark, silent and dim -
Mirkwood.
Cobwebs all around
Spooky silent and dim,
Deadly wild things,
Silent and dangerous.

Daniel Machin (9) Rise Park Junior School

DAFFODILS

Daffodils are bright
A leaf with a bee on
Flowers shut
Falling petals in the breeze
Orange stems
Dying stems
In the meadows
Long green stalks
Swaying in the breeze.

Emma Pyatt (8) & Samantha Bullock (7) Rufford Junior School

DAFFODILS

Daffodils grow fast and slow
Tall and small
Under trees in meadows
In the breeze
Tall stems
Waving about their pollen
Like powder
The most beautiful thing
Is their golden petals
Shining in the sun
I thought it was a beautiful sight.

Kayleigh Straw & Coral Davis (8) Rufford Junior School

DAFFODILS

Long green stems
Powdery pollen
Bright colours
Near the lake
Beneath the trees
Tall flowers
Yellow petals.

Ashley Robinson (7) Rufford Junior School

LOOK AT OUR WORLD

Have you cared to look at our world or maybe even sniffed?
Car fumes and rotten smells come from around
Factories should stop producing too much smoke.
The smoke pollutes our world and makes acid rain.
Have you cared to look at our world?

Gemma Shipman (11) Rufford Junior School

THE TWO DOVES

The two white doves sat perched in
the blossoming tree

They were like statues in the windy
tree with two black dots on their
necks

The white doves were beautiful

I turned my head and they were
gone

The tree stood on its own.

Peter Renwick (9) St Joseph's School

LOCH NESS

Is there something out there
  that we don't know about?
   Is there something creeping
    In there?
     A monster,
      Insect,
       Strange being
         Or even a UFO?
      We do not know.

Is there?
     Is there something out there -
  Lurking in the deep waters of Loch Ness?
   Something creepy
   Something weird -
Or is it the monster Nessie
         that everyone talks about?

So,
Is there?
Is there something out there
That we don't know about?

Felicity Youngson (10) St Joseph's School

200

WHITE POST FARM

We played on the tractor we fed the goats
Nibble! Nibble! Chomp!
We went in the owl-barn it was very dark.
Clanggg! I hit a pole
We went in a pig-barn and fed the pigs
After they ate - corr! What a stink!
We went round the pet stall
We saw the rabbits, dogs and hamsters
Then - 'arr' - lovely kittens
We went to stroke the rabbits
They had warm, lovely skin.
I had a go on the bikes that go the opposite way you turn,
Wibble Wobble off! I hit the ground.
Had a look at the horses
Fed them -
'Yuk' all sloppy
Then I said,
'Bye'
To all the animals
As we went home - bump, bump, bump.

Simon Kokoszko (9) St Joseph's School

CLIMBING UP THE FALLS

I feel excited and frightened to climb up Dunn's River Fall,
because I may slip.
But a guide is there to help us through the icy waters, to take
pictures, and show us the way.
As I climb up the rocks I see thousands of people down below.
People struggling to get on top of the Falls.
People trying to get onto a rock.
A woman with a video camera.
Higher, higher I climb over the rocks.
Through little pools of water.
I am now at the top and can see a sign saying
'The Falls finish here.'
On the dry land I go
after going through the last pool of water.
My shoes are soaked.
I take them off,
But I quickly put them on again
because the ground is too hot.
'That was a bit hard!' I say.
'When are we going to climb up the Falls again?'
'Oh!' groans everyone.
'Only kidding!' I reply.

Natasha Brown (10) St Joseph's School

WINTERTIME

The trees are bare as bare as can be,
Not a sound to be heard, not a sight to see,
The winter fog hides it all away,
Like a needle hidden in a bundle of hay.
The frost covers the whole of the ground,
Like a dust-covered old antique.
Then the frost would slowly melt away,
Until on the floor in puddles it lay.
Icicles glisten, dangling from the roofs,
Like witches' fingers but bigger and smooth.
Snowflakes falling from the fluffy white clouds,
And fall to the ground like drops of blood.
Then when the cockerel wakes us up,
The kids all gasp, 'Let's take a look,'
And what fills the sky but a storming blizzard,
That's more powerful than a wondrous wizard.
Then all of us go out and play,
But come in at the end of the day,
Then thinking of the day all through the night,
I feel so cold from the snowball fight,
Then I get up at 7 o'clock and guess what's
still there! It's the snow all white.
And a snowman's built and in goes the carrot,
It look like the beak of a daft old parrot.
On the very next day the sun will shine,
And will seem to suck it up as if to say,
'It's all mine.'
Then the frost glistens on the sparkling trees,
And I hear the buzzing of the old honey bees.

It's time for spring.

Lucy Daly (10) St Patrick's RC Primary School

THE SILVER POOL

The silver pool
With its glistening shine.
So calm and cool
Lost in time.
Overhanging silver birches
The distant sound of bells from churches.
Hearing the rustling of the bushes
While ducklings swim through the long green rushes.

As I sit by the pool my reflection I see
A familiar face staring back at me.
As on the green grass I lie
I look up into the bird filled sky.
Around the pool excited frogs leap
As if searching for treasure to keep.
As the little fish swim without coming to harm
I lie back and feel that the whole world is calm.

Claire Brown (11) St Philip Neri RC School

FLOWERS

Flowers swaying in the breeze
But at winter they do freeze,
Locked in a prison underground,
Then at springtime they are found
The shoot pushes its way free,
And when it blooms it attracts a bee,
But soon Jack Frost's army will attack again
And put an end to the flowers reign.

Eleanor Benton-Gunn (10) Sneinton C of E Primary School

SCHOOL DINNERS

At dinnertime I stay at school,
But the food is not always cool,
When there's chips on your plate,
You just can't wait,
Sometimes we have beans,
Sometimes we have greens,
When we have ice-cream,
It makes me beam
When we have jelly,
It wobbles in your belly,
When I drink milkshake,
It always gives me a headache,
But before I have my share,
I say a little prayer,
And after that,
I feel fat, and can't get off my chair!

Sarah Daoud (10) Sneinton C of E Primary School

OH NO!

There's a ghost on the stairs
And coming through the door
Oh no! There's
Greenies on the floor, with
Witches following closely and rats
Scurrying fast. There was
Blood all over, like
Red dripping fire balls.
There were mice, rats and
Spiders glaring from the
Cupboard.
Aarrggh!

Lee Morris (11) Sneinton C of E Primary School

205

OUTSIDE THE WINDOW

Outside the window the sun is shining brightly
A rainbow is underneath the sun
Outside the window the birds are chirping loudly
The rays from the sun are feeding the plants
Outside the window the flowers are radiant with colour
Early in the morning a blackbird sings a tune
Outside the window the trees are blowing against the wind
The wind is blowing the trees against the window
Outside the window an April shower begins
The rain is tapping on the window
Outside the window the colours are very dainty
The sun is setting very slowly
The colours are the colours of the rainbow
Outside the window are the colours visible
Reds, pinks, blues and greens of every shade and colour
Outside the window the sky is getting darker
The wind is getting stronger
Outside the window day has become night.

Sheli-Anne Robertson (11) Stevenson Junior School

A RIDDLE

I'm red but usually green
They have pips and they're usually mean
They're round and juicy sometimes fat
They squash very easily like a cat
Squashed I'll make lovely wine
Drink me and you'll be fine
When I'm dry you can put me in a cake
Put me in the oven I will bake

Who am I?   *Grape*

Shelley Thompson (9) Stevenson Junior School

206

MOON CAST SHADOWS

A night pitch black,
An old barn door creeks
And sways in the freezing cold wind.
Mysterious shadows are cast
Upon the old river lock.
Up above, the moonlight glows at night.
Creepy shapes and figures are appearing
Under small stone bridges.
Every now and then an owl
Coos or hoots in a large oak tree.
Headlights - one or two flicker
As they drive past me in the night.
Twelve o'clock, a pub clock strikes,
Shivers run up and down my spine,
Like ice cold fingers.

Richard Allum (10) Stevenson Junior School

OUTSIDE THE WINDOW

Outside the window the world lies
The wind blows the green grass
Outside the window enormous trees grow
With a bumpy brown bark and branches
                                    that stick out

Outside the window flowers sit
Their green shoots spring out
Outside the window hills roll
With animals making their residence.

Outside the window the sun still shines on
Its golden rays touch the earth
Outside the window is the deep blue sky
With fluffy white clouds hovering in the air.

Rebecca Thorpe (11) Stevenson Junior School

OUTSIDE THE WINDOW

Outside the window, the world goes by,
Outside the window, the wonder that meets the eye,
The green of the grass and the brightness of the flowers,
A world that you could watch for hours and hours.

The buds overhead, the badgers underground,
Squirrels are scurrying all around.
An army of ants walks round and round,
A little mole digging, makes a big, big mound.

The sun is now setting,
The sun's now gone down
The day creatures sleep,
The night ones come round.

Outside the window, the world grows dark,
Outside the window, there are new wonders to see,
The grass is now silver, and so are the flowers,
A world that will be moonlit, in the dark night-time hours.

The owls fly silently, the badgers emerge,
Mice and rats scurry, looking for food,
The bats flap along, in the dark night-time world,
The creatures of this time neither seen nor heard.

Jonathan Shierbaum (11) Stevenson Junior School

THE NIGHT WATCHER

Beneath fern, roots and weeds
A cat is sleeping,
His damp nose twitching,
His whiskers shivering.

Slowly arching his back with fright,
Moves gracefully, silently stepping round the garden,
His black coat shining in the pale moonlight.

Night watcher on the prowl.
He creeps around, jumps over the fence, walks down
the alley way,
His yellow, shiny eyes glaring round the corner of the street.
He saw the fish shop with the dim dark aspect inside,
And the old school house with the dreadful ghostly air,
He saw the blacksmith and the beach.

Night watcher on the prowl.
He squatted down
And closed his eyes to a slit -
glared.
The night watcher on the prowl.

Natalie Fisher (10) Stevenson Junior School

THE BUBBLE

Swoosh!
The wind twisted as
It blew
The small shiny
Bubble across the open
Field and over
The glittering golden
Stream, on a sparkling leaf
Where he had a nap
Suddenly!
There he was stuck
On the leaf for ever
And ever until he
Popped!
And splashed onto the
Floor.

Gareth Davies (11) Sunnyside Primary School

HOW TO MAKE A DOLPHIN

She needs . . .

Skin as smooth as silk,
Eyes as round as the sun
Gleaming on a hot summer's
      day,
Teeth as small and as sharp
      as pins,
A fin like a razor blade
      newly sharpened,
A whistle as squeaky as a
      mouse,
A click as quick as a
      cricket,
She swims like a whale
Softly and elegantly through
The bright blue sea.

Nicola Goodwin (10) Sunnyside Primary School

BUBBLES

Pop
Goes the bubble
As it shoots through the sky
Like an eagle watching
To eat whatever he finds
Like a glowing marble floating
Away like a feather
It flies
Higher and higher and
Until
Pop
Crackle

Look it's floating
Through the misty
Breeze
When will it pop
When will it cry for help
In the sky
It floats away.
When will it pray
For help
It strikes 12.00
Pop
And there was
A new city
Added to the land.

Gina Chapman (10) Sunnyside Primary School

WHERE DO ALL THE TEACHERS GO?

Where do all the teachers go
When it is 4 o'clock?
Do they live in houses;
And do they wash their socks?
Do they wear pyjamas,
And do they watch TV?
And do they pick their noses
Just like you and me?
Do they live with other people?
Have they mums and dads?
And were they ever children?
And were they ever bad?
Did they ever spell right?
Did they ever make mistakes?
Or get put in a corner,
Or pinch chocolate cakes?

Did they ever lose their hymn books
Did they ever leave their greens
Or scribble on their desks
Or wear some dirty jeans?
What, oh what, do teachers do,
When it's gone four o'clock.

Claire Dowson (11) Tuxford Primary School

CHRISTMAS CRACKER

Crackering Christmas spirits
Holly hung on the door
Robin perched on a twig
Ice skates on the floor
Santa comes to visit
And bring lovely presents and gifts
Time to get a Christmas tree
And decorate it nice
Mistletoe time is here
Time to be kissed have no fear
Apple pie so sweet is cooking in the oven
Sweets are coming too and some new shoes
Cracking Christmas cards
Reindeers come to my house at night
That's when we get a cracking fright
Apples so sweet and presents so neat
I just can't wait to eat eat eat
Candles lit at our lovely dinner
Just can't wait for that lovely supper
King of Our Saviour who gave us food and homes
Envelopes for Christmas cards and send them to our loved ones
Reindeer leave the houses tonight until another night.

Nicola Wyld (11) Tuxford Primary School

DREAMS

In your dreams you can fly,
In your dreams you can go anywhere you want
To space, unknown galaxies,
Make believe fairy tales come true.
Nightmares are different
Too scary for me
Vampires and monsters dominate your dreams.
In dreams you are sometimes rich,
And sometimes poor
You can live in a castle,
Or a tree house,
Or even in the sewers, (yuk!)
You can change into someone else
(Or something else!)
Your friends can come with you
Into your dreams.
You can find paradise with your family
But wherever you go
You always wake up!

Kim Barker (11) Tuxford Primary School

THE STORM

The storm thunders across the hills and valleys, destroying
everything in its path.
Boiling with rage the wind emits an almighty howl which echoes
around the great white peaked mountains.
The lightning's forked tongue reaches out into the old, dark night to snatch
whatever lies before it from the earth's grasp.
The thunder roars an evil laugh at the devastation it causes;
The raindrops begin to pound the earth like a drum, daring someone to
challenge it.
The storm is at its height now, raging, crashing and banging like never before.
People cringe and animals run for cover but no-one can escape her,
the storm, the anger of the night.

Francesca Pursell (11) Underwood C of E Primary School

THE CITY

Through the dark, unbroken world of the city,
By the train tracks, glistening bright,
I can see death before me,
Cold, dark and in pieces.
Round the mob of people, shops old and contaminated.
Beneath them the subways dark and dense.
Across rivers and ponds, drink cans lay cold and forgotten,
Through the dark, unbroken world of the city.
I can see death before me.

Laura Parsons (11) Walesby Primary School

BAD DAY

Get to school late
Everybody stares,
Pencils squeaking,
People whistling,
Oh! No!
Teacher shouting,
Sarah messing,
With her hair,
Yes at last,
Playtime,
Everybody playing,
Boys playing football,
Oh! No!
Ball's hit Debra,
Now she's crying,
Jade doing handstands,
There goes the whistle,
Everybody pushing,
To be first in line,
Oh! No!
Shaun and Richard fighting,
Quick teachers coming,
Be quiet!
People walking in,
Shh!
Be Quiet!
Silent reading,
Genevieve's fighting,
Over books,
Oh! No!
There goes Miss again,
Home time.

Amanda Yates (9) Whitemoor Primary School

HERE COME THE ALIENS

In outer space it's black as night
And something's moving at the speed of light
Something's looking for a fight
The aliens are coming.

Twinkle twinkle little star
The aliens are coming.

None speak English French or Greek.
They sort of grunt burp or squeak.
The aliens are slowing.

Approaching Earth they see
A piece of paper floating free.
Though how it got there don't ask me.
For this is what the aliens saw
A picture of your class aged 4.
It scared them off of their way.

The aliens are going
Yes the aliens agree
Of every life in every galaxy
The ugliest are you and me.

The aliens are gone, vamoosed.
The aliens have gone.

Sunita Landa (9) Whitemoor Primary School

SUMMER

The summer season is full of adventure.
Children buying ice-creams having fun
Everyone's happy
The best thing I like about summer
Is that the bright sun is out
And when the summer goes away
I know that the next day
It will come again.
Thank you for being the best summer.

Mahezabin Hirani (9) Whitemoor Primary School

THE CIRCUS

Hooray! Hooray! It is the circus today.
There will be laughing juggling and all
sorts today,
Hooray! Hooray! It is the circus today.
Come on! Come on! Lets get into the car
lets zoom, lets zoom, until we are there.
Flashing lights, flashing lights, red, green and blue,
Oh look, oh look, two seats, two seats, two seats,
two seats for me and you.
Brilliant, brilliant, brilliant, do it again,
don't end, don't end, don't end, not yet.
Clap, clap, clap, clap, bye, bye, bye, bye.
What a wonderful day.

Amy Stewart (9) Willow Farm Primary School

SPRING POEM

All the eggs are hatching
here there and everywhere
all the animals are out of hibernation.
The birds are singing all day.
It's Easter in 2 whole weeks, and I'm
getting impatient.
The foxes who are in my garden,
have had another six cubs.
The world seems to be filled
with spring beauty.

Holly Swaby (8) Willow Farm Primary School

THE SUN IS SHINING

The sun is shining,
The sky is blue,
And I feel happy,
Happy all through.

The birds are flying,
The sky is blue,
It's good to be happy,
Happy all through.

The flowers are dancing,
The sky is blue,
It's lovely to be happy,
Happy all through.

The sun is shining,
The sky is blue,
And I feel happy,
Happy all through.

Heather Salmon (8) Willow Farm Primary School

UNTITLED

Spring is here again at last,
the flowers and plants all grow very fast.
Birds and butterflies, bumble bees,
fly around the plants and trees.

The warm spring sunshine,
the soft spring rain,
splashing in puddles,
it runs down the drain,
I'm happy spring is here again.

Leanne Mathieson (7) Willow Farm Primary School

AUTUMN IS . . .

Spiky hedgehogs crawling silently on the
soft green grass.
Conkers on the crispy leaves.
Squirrels gathering nuts for hibernation
in winter.
Cars skidding on the icy ground.
Bare branches on the trees blowing
in the wind.
Days getting shorter and nights getting
longer.

Laura Hollingworth (9) Willow Farm Primary School

INFORMATION

We hope you have enjoyed reading this book - and that you will continue to enjoy it in the coming years.

If you like reading and writing poetry drop us a line, or give us a call, and we'll send you a free information pack.

Write to

Young Writers Information
1-2 Wainman Road
Woodston
Peterborough
PE2 7BU